WAR
BABIES

For The Silent Generation

WAR
BABIES

CHRIS MANBY &
SIMON ROBINSON

MIRROR BOOKS

MIRROR BOOKS

1

Published in Great Britain and Ireland in 2025 by
Mirror Books, a Reach PLC business.

www.mirrorbooks.co.uk
@TheMirrorBooks

Print ISBN 9781917439480
eBook ISBN 9781917439497

Editing and Production: Christine Costello
Cover Design: Chris Collins

Photographic Acknowledgements: Alamy, MirrorPix, the personal collections of all interviewees

Every effort has been made to trace copyright, Any oversights will be rectified in future editions.

Printed and bound in Great Britain by
CPI Group (UK) Ltd, Croydon, CR0 4YY

MIX
Paper | Supporting
responsible forestry
FSC® C013604

CONTENTS

CONTENTS

AUTHORS' NOTE

IN 2025, 80 YEARS AFTER the end of World War Two, we celebrated the remaining Allied veterans who served their countries with great selflessness and bravery between 1939 and 1945. But those men and women who donned uniforms to 'do their bit' were not the only people affected by the conflict that turned much of the world upside down. Many millions of children also lived through the war. Alongside their parents and grandparents, aunts, uncles, older siblings and friends, they too lived on rations, faced the bombs and were, in many terrible cases, imprisoned, subjected to torture and used as slave labour. Though the children of World War Two were too young to serve they were not too young to suffer, both small privations and great tragedy.

During the past year, we have been lucky enough to meet some of those children and talk to them about their wartime experiences: from the thrill of seeing the countryside for the first time upon being evacuated and the excitement of meeting the American GIs, to the terror of the Blitz and the deep sadness of losing loved ones to the conflict, both on the front line and at home.

We're very grateful to the men and women you will meet in these pages for joining us to look back over what were sometimes painful memories and agreeing to share them here. The generation that went to war in 1939 has been called *The Greatest Generation*. Those people born between 1928 and 1945, were dubbed *The Silent Generation*. Now it's time for The Silent Generation to be heard.

Chris Manby and Simon Robinson. London, 2025

WORLD WAR TWO BEGINS

'This country is at war...'

SEPTEMBER 3RD 1939 IS A day that will live forever in the memories of those who were old enough to be allowed to listen to the 'important announcement' the BBC promised its listeners on the morning news. After the events of the previous few days, most adults must have guessed what they were about to be told. At 11.15am the Conservative Prime Minister Neville Chamberlain finally came on air to put the people of the United Kingdom out of their misery. Or rather, straight into it.

In sombre tones, Prime Minister Chamberlain began, 'This morning the British Ambassador in Berlin handed the German Government a final note, stating that unless we heard from them by 11 o'clock that they were prepared at once to withdraw their troops from Poland, a state of war would exist between us. I have to tell you now that no such undertaking has been received, and that consequently this country is at war with Germany.'

The earnest efforts of Chamberlain's government to avert another European war had come to nothing. Chamberlain's famous September 30th 1938 speech, regarding the Munich Agreement, in which he proclaimed that he had brokered 'peace for our time', was but a distant memory. Despite Adolf Hitler's promise that he would make no more territorial demands in Europe, the leader of Nazi Germany had done exactly as he pleased. Hitler had invaded Poland and, due to a mutual assistance agreement, Britain was obliged to go to Poland's defence.

The outbreak of the First World War – the Great War – had been met with a degree of patriotic enthusiasm. This time, the feeling was very different. The huge number of casualties the Great War had exacted – nearly every family lost a loved one – had shocked even the most hardened warmongers. Now, up and down the country, as Britain braced for war again, the adults were at best resigned. Many were desperate.

On September 3rd, having told the British people they were at war, Chamberlain continued, 'We have a clear conscience. We have done all that any country could do to establish peace. But the situation in which no word given by Germany's ruler could be trusted, and no people or country could feel itself safe, had become intolerable. And now that we have resolved to finish it, I know that you will all play your part with calmness and courage.'

Chamberlain's 'all' included Britain's estimated seven million under-14s. But as small children all over the United Kingdom fired catapults at imaginary German paratroopers, they had no idea how the coming war would affect them and define the rest of their lives.

OPERATION PIED PIPER

'Out of Harm's Way'

THOUGH THE BRITISH GOVERNMENT HAD tried to prevent war by diplomatic means up until the very last moment, preparations for conflict with Germany had actually been going on for some time. Everyone understood that this new war would be different to the last. Advances in military technology meant that warfare was no longer mostly confined to old-fashioned front lines where only military personnel were under fire. Air power was much more advanced now, making the English Channel no obstacle for a determined enemy. It was fully expected that air raids would target British civilians and that they would begin at any moment.

The Germans had used gas extensively during the Great War and there was no reason to think they wouldn't do so again. Before Chamberlain's 1938 meeting with Hitler in Munich, more than 35 million gas masks were handed out to the public. These included bright red and blue 'Mickey Mouse' masks for small children. It was hoped the cartoonish design might make putting on a mask less frightening. At the same time, air raid shelters were constructed up and down the country and night-time blackouts were planned. Leaflets were distributed to every household, explaining what would be expected of the general public should war be declared.

Britain had already welcomed a number of young refugees fleeing conflict in mainland Europe. They included some 4,000 children, nicknamed the 'Ninos', escaping the civil war in Spain. They were followed in 1938 and early 1939 by almost 10,000 Jewish children, fleeing Nazi persecution in Germany, Austria and Czechoslovakia.

The 'Kindertransport' programme was implemented in response to *Kristallnacht*, the Night of Broken Glass, of November 9-10th 1938, when the Nazi Party's paramilitaries and some of their civilian supporters attacked Jewish homes and businesses. The evacuation scheme was supported by the British government, which waived visa requirements for child refugees without documents to hurry along their flight to safety.

With the Kindertransport underway, the idea that children might one day also need to be evacuated from Britain's cities was tabled by the Anderson Committee under the leadership of Scottish politician Sir John Anderson (who would also give his name to the Anderson air raid shelters – the corrugated steel structures that were appearing in gardens up and down the country). The Committee put together a plan to be carried out by the Ministry of Health and Operation Pied Piper was born.

The Anderson Committee divided England and Wales into three categories: Evacuation, Neutral and Reception. Evacuation areas were those parts of the country deemed most at risk from aerial bombardment. Neutral areas were those at a lower risk and Reception areas were those considered safe enough to accept children who had to be moved.

Once the categories had been decided, the Committee carried out a survey of available housing in the reception areas. The National Camps Corporation was commissioned to build 30 residential camps to provide city children with the opportunity to spend time in the countryside, but which could also be quickly repurposed as accommodation for evacuees. Early 1939 saw some small-scale evacuation of England's children. Among the first cohort were children with disabilities and special educational needs.

Meanwhile Scotland drew up its own evacuation scheme, designating big cities such as Dundee, Edinburgh and Glasgow as 'sending areas', whose vulnerable children would be sent to 'receiving areas' in less highly-populated regions such as the Highlands and Kincardineshire. Northern Ireland would also make its own plans, though not until the summer of 1940 when the Germans occupied France and it was clear that enemy planes would be able to reach Belfast too.

Though it was decided that evacuation would not be compulsory, a propaganda campaign encouraged parents to sign up to the scheme through their children's schools. The campaign worked very well indeed. Most parents in the evacuation areas wanted their children to be out of harm's way and initial take-up for the scheme was enormous.

At the start of August 1939, schools in the evacuation zones began practice drills. Evacuees-in-waiting would muster at their schools with their suitcases, rucksacks and gas masks, with their names and home addresses written on labels that were pinned to their clothes. Once the children were assembled, they would march to the bus stops and rail stations from which their evacuation transports would depart if the official order was given.

That order finally came on the evening of Thursday August 31st 1939. *Operation Pied Piper* went into action the following morning.

During the first three days of Operation Pied Piper, more than 600,000 children were evacuated.

Many of the children travelled as schools, along with their teachers, on specially chartered trains. But as they waved goodbye to their families, most had no idea what might await them at the end of their journey. Parents would have to wait for a postcard to arrive several days or even weeks later with their children's new addresses. All they could do in the meantime was trust that in letting their precious sons and daughters go to live with strangers, they were doing the right thing.

On arriving at their destinations, some children were met by organised reception teams, often overseen by the Women's Voluntary Service, the WVS, which had already decided who would be billeted where (though the best laid plans often went awry when more children than expected turned up). Other evacuated children faced something akin to a Roman slave market, with foster families picking out prospective charges willy-nilly, hoping perhaps for extra help around the house or on the farm, until only the weaker-looking children remained. Some foster families wanted only girls. Others wanted only boys. To their horror, siblings were not always able to stay together.

There was often an immediate culture clash between the city children and their country hosts. Some foster families were horrified by the city children's low standards of hygiene. Many of the evacuees had come from desperately poor backgrounds and did not have the tough clothes and boots they would need for a country life. Indeed, some arrived with their meagre belongings not in suitcases but in paper bags. At the same time, some of the wealthier evacuees found they had been billeted in remote farms that had none of the conveniences, such as indoor bathrooms and electric light, that they had been used to back in the city. They were shocked to learn that they'd have to take baths in a tub in the middle of the kitchen.

An apocryphal story of the time illustrates the gulf between town and country children. An East End boy, sharing a room with a country lad, woke on his first night to a weird sound that filled him with terror. His room-mate assured him that it was 'only an owl' to which the Londoner is said to have replied, 'Yeah mate, I knows that, but 'oo the 'eck 'owled?'

As they bedded down in their new homes on what was often the first night the evacuees had ever spent away from their families, how must those brave young children have felt? Children like six-year-old Jean Kent, who was sent from North London to rural Berkshire...

Jean Kent, 93

WHEN I HEARD THE NEWS that my brother Kenny and I were being evacuated to the countryside, I was excited. I don't remember feeling worried at all. It seemed like a big adventure to me. We left North London on a sunny day at the end of the summer and were taken to Mortimer, a village not far from Reading.

My family came from Wood Green, just up the road from the Bounds Green tube station. My father was a publican and my mother was a housewife. I was the youngest of four children. We were a spread-out family. My sister Winnie – the eldest – was 17 years older than me. Then came my two brothers. Fred was ten years my senior and Kenny was already five when I was born.

Kenny was the one I spent most time with because once I was big enough our mother would make him take me with him whenever he went out to play. He'd always complain – 'Do I have to?' – but he would do as he was told and I'd tag along to the park. He'd look after me all day and how would I repay him? When we were about two minutes away from home, I'd start howling, then, as soon as we got in, I'd tell Mum, 'Kenny hit me with a ball!' or something like that. I wasn't a very nice child, I think.

Home was a flat on the first floor of a big house. We shared a bathroom with the other families in the building. You had to put a penny in the geyser to get hot water. In 1939, a bomb shelter was put up in the garden for everyone to use – an Anderson shelter – but once the war started my parents decided it was best for me and Kenny, being the two youngest, to be evacuated. As I understand it, my parents would have to pay a bit each week for our keep and the government would pay the rest. My sister and my older brother were already both at work. Winnie was working in an office and Fred was an apprentice to a carpenter.

Kenny was with me for the journey from London but when we got to Mortimer, we were split up and sent to stay with different families. I don't think he minded too much. By this time, I was seven and he was 12, so he was glad not to have to look after me. I wasn't on my own though. I went with my friend Eileen, who was the same age as me, to stay with Mr and Mrs Dolley.

The Dolleys were an older couple whose own children, six girls, had all grown up and left home. They didn't have a choice when it came to taking in evacuees – like the rest of the village, they'd been told they had to find room for us – but having raised six daughters, Mrs Dolley insisted she had to have girls. She told the people organising the billeting, 'You can't give me boys. I won't know how to mend their britches.'

Mr and Mrs Dolley lived in Holly Cottage, one of two adjoining cottages about a mile and a half from the centre of the village. Holly Cottage was very small. There were two bedrooms and three other rooms: a parlour, which is what they called the sitting room, a kitchen with an open fire, which was where we spent most of our time, and the scullery. That was where the sink was. There was no fitted kitchen. Mrs Dolley had a little electric cooker which stood on a table.

There was no bathroom at Holly Cottage either. There was an outdoor toilet and baths were taken in a tin tub in front of the kitchen fire. The house wasn't even connected to the water mains.

All the water from the scullery drained into a large container outside which Mr Dolley had to empty with a ladle and bucket. He then carried the waste water to the top of the garden. It was the same with the toilet!

On wash day, Mrs Dolley would fill the copper in the scullery with water and light a fire beneath it. Clothes soaked in the hot water for a while before being transferred to the sink where they were rubbed with a scrubbing brush on a corrugated board. Mrs Dolley had a sort of hand-washing machine, a tub with a blade underneath that you turned to agitate the washing inside. If it was a nice day, she would take the whites out into the garden and spread them across the hedge to bleach in the sunlight as they dried.

Ironing was done with old fashioned flat irons made from heavy cast iron. Electric irons were still very expensive. Mrs Dolley didn't have an ironing board so she would lay a blanket and sheet on the table and work on that. She would have two irons on the go. She would be pressing clothes with one, while the other was heating up on the fire. When the iron she was using got too cool, she would swap it for the freshly heated one and keep on like that until she finished.

Eileen and I were given chores. My favourite was polishing the brass tap. I would also help bring in logs for the fire, carrying them in the skirt of my pinny. And every day I'd go to the shop to pick up the evening paper. At the same time, I'd collect copies for our neighbours, Mrs Parsons and Mrs Bushnell. For that errand, I earned 6d a week. When Mr and Mrs Dolley had finished reading the news, I had the job of cutting the paper into squares to be used in the loo. Looking back, Eileen and I didn't have to do too much about the house but Mrs Dolley was very good at teaching us things that would be useful to know when we were adults.

Mr Dolley was head forester on the Benyon Estate, where they grew fir trees for telegraph poles. At home he grew fruit and vegetables. We never had to go to the shop for those. We ate whatever was in season. You ate peas until the peas ran out, then broad beans until they were finished, etc. Throughout the growing season, Mr Dolley laid down stores of carrots, beetroot and potatoes to last us through the winter. I loved beetroot and potatoes. Because Mr and Mrs Dolley saw how much I loved them, I would always get extra mash.

When we had potatoes, Mrs Dolley would wash the peelings, pat them dry and wrap them in newspaper. I'd take the dried-out peelings across the road to our neighbours who kept rabbits. I loved feeding the rabbits, though I suppose they were being raised for food. Back at home, Mr Dolley had a dog, a terrier called Monty because his black and white markings made it look as though he was wearing a beret, like Field Marshall Montgomery.

The Dolleys were very kind to me and Eileen, as were the rest of the villagers, and we soon fitted in. We had lessons at the village school, St Mary's Church of England. We went to Sunday school and I joined the Brownies. I enjoyed school. The headmaster was a pleasant man. There were two older female teachers who were less friendly – if you were naughty, one of them had a way of tapping you sharply on the top of your arm that would sting for ages afterwards – but I liked learning and especially enjoyed religious knowledge. Back in Wood Green, I'd been fascinated by our family Bible, which seemed gigantic to me as a child. I remember Mum showing the Bible to me and telling me that when I turned 13, I would have it for my own.

I recall that once a year, we had a Bible knowledge exam at school. The year I arrived in Mortimer, I came second in the test, but because the boy who came first had won the prize the previous year, it was awarded to me instead. I'll never forget that.

For as long as I can remember, one of my favourite pastimes was reading. I would read anything I could get my hands on. I was very envious of another evacuee I knew who had a bookcase in her room at the house where she was staying. Then someone in the village set up a makeshift library. They made a table by putting a plank across two stools and laid books out all across it and we'd pay a penny to borrow a book for a week. I read all the Enid Blyton books. I also remember reading *Uncle Tom's Cabin* by Harriet Beecher Stowe. That story made me cry and cry.

At school, we learned how to dance around the maypole for May Day. I was always very concerned for Colin Ems, a small boy from my class whose job was to sit at the bottom of the maypole to keep it steady, while we danced around him with our ribbons. He was very nicely dressed with velvet trousers and it didn't seem right that he had to sit on the floor. Also in May was Empire Day, when a flagpole was put up in the playing field and we had to march around it with small flags representing the various nations in the British Empire.

I remember one special school trip which happened later in the war. We were taken on a bus to Reading to go to an orchestral concert, conducted by John Barbirolli, the former conductor of the New York Philharmonic, who returned to England to lead Manchester's Halle Orchestra. They played Prokofiev's 'Peter and The Wolf' and I was enthralled. Barbirolli explained how Prokofiev had created the personality of each character through the music. Later, we all sang together and the feeling of the hall filled with the sound of children singing was just wonderful.

In the evenings at Holly Cottage, we would gather round the wireless in the kitchen for *Children's Hour*. I loved to hear the stories about Mompty the Cat and Peckham the Dog. I think Mr Dolley secretly enjoyed listening in too. We didn't listen to the news so the war felt far away even though there was a prisoner of war camp near the village, housing Italian PoWs.

In May 1940, after the Netherlands was occupied by the Germans, Queen Wilhemina escaped to England. She came to live in Mortimer too. We'd sometimes see her around the village in her long brown coat. She brought with her Doctor Kootman, her personal doctor, who joined the local GP practice. He was very popular. You'd go to the surgery and everyone would be waiting for him.

The Dolleys did their best to make me and Eileen feel at home. I loved staying with them but Eileen was homesick and wanted to go back to London, especially after a visit from her parents. Mum came to see me and my brother too but she was sure that the country was the best place for us and wouldn't let us come home. I can remember only one occasion when I cried about being away from Wood Green.

We didn't know much about what was going on back in London. Mr and Mrs Dolley didn't want to frighten us with things we didn't need to know. All the same, in the autumn of 1940, Eileen and I must have had an inkling that the war was getting worse. I remember becoming aware that something horrible had happened to the cathedral in Coventry but I still didn't know that any bombs had been dropped on London.

One night around that time, after Eileen and I went to bed, we noticed that Mr and Mrs Dolley had closed the kitchen door. That was unusual. We could hear their muffled voices and immediately decided they must be talking about something that wasn't for children's ears. Naturally, that made us curious, so we got out of bed and crept to the kitchen door to eavesdrop. We soon wished we hadn't. They were talking about London.

'London's got it badly tonight,' said Mr Dolley. Apparently, you could see the fires burning in the East End from miles around. Eileen and I quickly got back into bed before Mr and Mrs Dolley found us listening.

A couple of days later, Mrs Dolley collected me from school. That was unusual. I usually walked home with Eileen and other children. Mrs Dolley didn't say anything as we walked home. When we got to Holly Cottage, she sat me down at the table and gave me a new cut-out book. She said, 'Now you sit there, be a good girl and do that.' I was surprised and pleased, but then she told me, 'Your mother's been killed, Jean. And your sister.'

I sat there, looking at my new book, not knowing what to say. Mrs Dolley didn't seem to know what to say either. She didn't put her arms around me or anything like that. It wasn't the way of her generation. But that was how I found out that my mum and my sister Winnie had died on November 1st 1940. Mum was 47. Winnie was 24.

I don't remember anything more being said about it after that. I quickly got the impression it was something to be embarrassed about. I never lost that feeling. In years to come, if anyone asked about my mum or my sister, I would quickly say, 'They were killed in the Blitz,' and leave it there. That thought stayed with me – that it was something to be ashamed of – right through my childhood and for years afterwards. It was something we just didn't talk about.

I later found out that Mum and Winnie had gone down to the Anderson shelter in the garden when the air raid started. Dad and my older brother were both out at work. A German pilot dropped a bomb on the shelter which exploded with such force that it almost brought the house where our flat was down too. All the same, as I understand it, if Mum and Winnie had been in the flat that night, rather than the shelter, they might have survived.

Eileen went back to London but there was no question of me doing the same now. There was nowhere for me to go back to. Dad went to live in the hotel where he was working.

Even though my brother Kenny was just down the road in Mortimer, I wasn't taken to see him the day we found out Mum and Winnie died. We didn't ever talk about it between ourselves. Dad never mentioned them. But other family members – aunts and uncles – did send presents. I remember receiving a beautiful doll's pram.

There weren't many personal things left from the family home for me to remember Mum and Winnie by. A little later, I was given Mum's engagement ring and a small glass perfume bottle. I passed Mum's ring onto my daughter and I still have the perfume bottle. I don't know what happened to the family Bible Mum had shown me all those years before. It must have been destroyed in the bombing.

We didn't see much of Dad. He was always working, though he came to Mortimer whenever he could. On the days he was coming, I would wait for him at the gate, knowing he would always be on the midday or the 12.15 bus.

During the school summer holidays, I went to stay with relatives on their farm at Syleham near Diss in Norfolk, just as my sister had done when she was a child. Mrs Dolley would put me on the bus to Reading where Dad would meet me for the train ride to London. He'd then put me on another train to Norfolk. We'd find the ladies' carriage and Dad would give a train guard a couple of bob to keep an eye on me until I reached my destination, where my aunts would be waiting on the platform. Dad had three sisters and three brothers and they all lived around the same village. My grandfather had been a blacksmith there.

I was always a little homesick at first but I did enjoy those summers in Norfolk. When I first started going there, my relatives on the farm didn't have a tractor, just horses. I'd stretch out on straw in the back of the cart and hang on tightly while we went bumping down the lanes. Later, when my uncle did get a tractor, he taught me how to drive it. It wasn't difficult. You just had to keep the front wheels in line with the corn that had already been cut.

My uncle also ran a pub called the White Horse Inn. Nearby was an air base, the Thorpe Abbotts airfield, where men from the United

States Air Force were stationed. We got used to seeing American airmen around the pub. They were very friendly. There were two in particular who became close with my aunt and uncle. Gene and Ray, they were called. I think they were bomber pilots, both about 21 years old. They were always together. They'd come over and sit out in the orchard behind the pub, chatting and laughing with my relatives, while I listened from my hammock between two trees. I liked Gene and Ray very much. It must have been a relief for them to be able to relax with my family after the seriousness of their work.

Then one night Gene stopped by on his own and I could tell at once that something was different. He told my uncle, 'Ray didn't come back last night.' I didn't know what he meant, where Ray hadn't come back from, but of course he must have been shot down during a mission over Germany. We didn't talk about Ray again. It was just like with Mum and Winnie. Talking about death was embarrassing. We just had to get on with living. But I do remember thinking that it wasn't right that men as young as Ray were dying in the war.

After Mum died, my aunts in Norfolk wanted me to come and live with them full-time but I didn't want that and I was pretty stubborn about it. I wanted to go back to Mortimer to live with Mr and Mrs Dolley. I liked my life there, with school and the Brownies.

It does seem incredible now that no-one talked to me about losing my mother and sister, but people in Mortimer showed their kindness in other ways. Mr Dolley had a shed at the bottom of the garden. It didn't have a door. He hung a swing from a beam in the shed's roof for me and, when I wanted to be on my own, I would go and sit there.

As it got close to November 1941 and the first anniversary of Mum and Winnie's deaths, the Brownies were preparing for Remembrance Sunday and church parade. At the end of the parade, one of us would lay a wreath at the war memorial. Brown Owl had us all stand in a circle, then closed her eyes and spun round a couple of times before coming to a standstill, pointing at the girl who would have the honour. She pretended she had chosen me at random but I knew that she meant to land on me. I was very happy until the vicar's wife said, 'She can't lay the wreath because she hasn't got a uniform,' to which Brown Owl snapped back, 'She can lay the wreath without a uniform and she will.'

As I got older, I would sometimes help Mr Dolley with his work. He had a number of men working under him on the Benyon Estate and, on a Thursday evening, he'd draw up a time sheet, filling in the names of his team members, the hours they'd worked and the duties they had undertaken, ready to be taken to the estate office on Friday morning. On Fridays, Mr Dolley would put on his freshly-polished gaiters to look his best when he went to meet his employer and collect the wages for all his men. On Saturday mornings, Mr Dolley would deliver pensions to former estate workers who were now retired. They lived in estate cottages rent-free and in addition to their pension, they also received free logs.

One Saturday, Mr Dolley was unwell and he entrusted the job of delivering the pensions to me. I remember how carefully I carried his leather purse, filled with half crowns, to the three pensioners who lived in Mortimer. After that, taking the pensions round on a Saturday became my job.

When I first came to Mortimer, Mr Dolley would go to work on a bicycle. He rode so slowly that the local children would joke when they saw him, 'Here comes Mr Dolley, tacking along on his sewing machine.'

Eventually he got himself a low-powered motorbike, so he could get around more quickly. At the end of the day, I would listen out for the motorbike's engine as he came down the road. When I heard it, I'd run to open the garden gate, then I'd jump on the pillion seat and Mr Dolley would drive me slowly up the garden path.

After the war ended, I stayed on in Mortimer because I still didn't have a home to go back to. Our flat in Wood Green had been demolished. Dad was still living in the hotel. Besides, I liked living with Mr and Mrs Dolley. It was decided that I would stay with them until I finished school.

I left school at 14 because that's what you did back then. You left school and started to pay your way. I came back to London to live with an aunt and uncle and got my first job in a chemist's shop. Later, I worked at a factory and then found a position as a telephonist at the GPO. After four years of that, I took up a clerical role in telephone accounts. I met my husband George through my cousin. He was best friends with her fiancé. When George and I got married, we moved in with his mother south of the river.

I kept in touch with Mr and Mrs Dolley for many years. When my children, Alison and George, were born, I made sure to take them to Mortimer. When Mr and Mrs Dolley passed away, I stayed in touch with their daughters, whom I'd come to think of as aunts.

Looking back I can see that the war affected me very much and still does. Watching the news on Holocaust Memorial Day this year brought it all back. I remembered going to the cinema towards the end of the war and between two films, on the *Pathe Gazette* news, we saw footage of the liberation of the concentration camps. It was so terrible, I could hardly believe it. How could people be so cruel? And yet we have to be reminded of it even now. There's always hatred there. Some people have to hate someone.

What impression remembering these things has on the younger generation, I don't know. They've got their own problems. Things are hard today in a different way. I don't envy anyone trying to bring their children up on the straight and narrow now, but that's another story, isn't it?

I've decided that I can't keep going over the past. I've got to look forward and make the most of the time I have left with my loved ones. My children had children of their own and I have several great-grandchildren now. I'm an active member of my local church. I believe my mother was a Christian and her faith has inspired mine. I feel very lucky to have my family, my friends and my faith.

3

SHORTAGES, RATIONING AND *SNOEK*

'Yes, we have no bananas...'

JUST AS OPERATION PIED PIPER had been in the pipeline for some time, so the British Government had been planning for several years how it would feed its citizens if worst came to worst.

Even in the 1930s, the United Kingdom was not self-sufficient but was a net importer of food. In 1939, the UK produced only a third of the produce it consumed. During peacetime, this had not been a problem. However, it was obvious that international conflict might disturb the smooth supply of food from overseas.

In the summer of 1939, as war with Germany started to look like an inevitability, the Ministry of Food printed 50 million ration books – one for every man, woman and child. On January 8th 1940, those careful preparations came to fruition when the Ministry introduced the first food rationing, setting limits on sugar, butter and bacon.

The ration books contained coupons, to be handed over when buying rationed goods. Other less basic items, such as biscuits, would be allocated using a points system. Each household had to register with specific retailers, who would be stocked with only enough food for their registered customers. Price controls were also put in place to make certain that everyone got their fair share, no matter how rich or how poor. Eggs, for example, were subsidised.

Not everything was rationed. To stave off morale-sapping hunger, bread and potatoes were not subject to limits (though, ironically, bread would go 'on the ration' in 1946, after the war had ended). Though meat quickly became very hard to come by, no limits were imposed on fish. And you could buy as much fruit and veg as you liked, if you could find it... As the whisper went round that a certain shop had a certain item, a queue would hurriedly form as people rushed to get hold of something good before the shelves were bare again.

Bananas were suddenly as rare as unicorns, bringing a new poignancy to the famous 1920's novelty song, 'Yes! We Have No Bananas'. When oranges were available, they were reserved for children under five.

To combat some of the shortages, people were encouraged to grow their own fruit and vegetables at home. For those who didn't have a garden or an allotment, a number of parks were turned over to the public for the purpose of growing food, under a scheme with the slogan 'Dig For Victory'. Even the moat around the Tower of London was given over to growing veg.

To ensure everyone had what they needed, the Ministry devised a scheme to allocate rations on the basis of the recipient's age and profession. Manual labourers would need more than office workers. The sick would need extra food to help them recover their health. Pregnant women and nursing mothers received a larger ration of milk. Children had smaller rations than adults but they were given proportionally more protein and fat to aid growth.

To ensure the health of the nation's children, the government also provided very cheap or free food supplements. One of those supplements was Haliborange, halibut liver oil mixed with orange juice. Lucky children had a spoonful of this every morning. At the end of the day, they would be given a spoonful of malt, a thick brown treacle-like substance extracted from grain that was high in Vitamin A, for good growth, and riboflavin to protect against anaemia. Kepler's, which combined malt with cod liver oil, was a popular brand, as was Radio Malt. Both brands contained calciferol, a form of Vitamin D.

With the addition of supplements like Haliborange and Radio Malt, it's likely that many children from poorer families actually ended up having a healthier diet during the war than they'd had before. Rickets, a weakening of the bones caused by a deficiency of vitamin D, which makes sufferers bow-legged, was largely eradicated thanks to wartime supplementation. All the same, the rations were not nearly enough to grow fat on. It's said that when Churchill was shown a photograph of the average family's rations, he said to his ministers, 'Well, that looks like a decent enough meal to me.' He had no idea that the food he had taken to represent one good meal was supposed to last a family of four a whole week. When rationing was at its most strict, the typical weekly allowance included just one ounce of cheese and four ounces of bacon or ham.

You could eat that cheese and ham with as much bread as you liked, but to make sure bread was always available, the Federation of Bakers introduced a 'National Loaf', a wholemeal loaf fortified with vitamins and calcium, designed to be produced with less waste than white bread. At the same time, the government introduced a very unusual measure to make sure no-one ate their daily bread too casually. It was decreed that bread could not be sold fresh but could only be sold the day *after* baking, when it had lost its tempting freshly baked smell and was easier to slice more thinly.

The National Loaf was deeply unpopular but it was also a great leveller. It was even served to the American President Roosevelt's wife when she visited Buckingham Palace in 1942. Mrs Roosevelt wrote in her diary, 'We were served on gold and silver plates, but our bread was the same kind of war bread any other family had to eat.'

The Ministry of Food did its best to encourage the British to make the most of their rations with poster and leaflet campaigns. One of those campaigns starred Potato Pete, a talking spud, who smiled out from leaflets containing jolly rhymes such as, *'Potatoes new, potatoes old, potato (in a salad) cold... Enjoy them all including chips, Remembering spuds don't come in ships.'*

While the Battle of the Atlantic raged, it was significant that potatoes did not have to be imported. Their ready availability didn't mean that anyone could afford to waste them however, as this other rhyme reminded Britain's cooks: *'Those who have the will to win, cook potatoes in their skin, knowing that the sight of peelings, deeply hurts Lord Woolton's feelings.'*

Lord Woolton was the Minister of Food and surprisingly popular considering he oversaw rationing. He even had a pie named after him – Woolton Pie – the recipe for which stood as a perfect example of how to eat well in wartime. It was a pie with a pastry or potato crust, with a filling of parsnips, carrots, turnips, oatmeal and potatoes – no meat – made *almost* tasty with brown gravy.

They say that necessity is the mother of invention and food rationing certainly required the cooks of Great Britain to get creative. They were encouraged by celebrity cooks such as Marguerite Patten, who gave cooking advice to the Home Service on a programme called *The Kitchen Front*. She made tours of hospitals and factory canteens, where she would demonstrate in person how to successfully use new ingredients such as powdered eggs, reconstituted with water. A stomach-turning mixture of margarine, milk and cornflour could be substituted for cream. Carrots could be swapped for sugar. Patten even invented a Christmas recipe called 'Mock Goose'. Naturally, it contained no goose. It was made from lentils, sage and breadcrumbs.

It wasn't only goose that had to be substituted. Tinned meat such as spam was popular with Britain's children but one other tinned food was decidedly less so. This was SNOEK (pronounced Snook), which was the name of the South African pike-like fish from which it was made. At least, that's what it was supposed to be made from. A rumour went around that it was actually made from whale. A Giles cartoon in the *Daily Express* showed the Giles family preparing to open a tin – Ma with tin opener and Pa standing by with an axe in case the contents attacked them.

Certainly, the Ministry of Food really did attempt to convince people that they should try whale meat. It was 'off ration'. But evidently the British public decided it would rather go without than eat whale and in the end it was largely used for cat and dog food.

Surprising as it seems – and luckily for our war babies – at the beginning of World War Two, chocolate was considered an essential food. In newspaper advertisements in 1940, Cadbury's announced, *'If it's chocolate, it's food. Cadbury's Milk Chocolate has all the three food properties which the Ministry of Food are urging us to include in our daily diet.'*

Cadbury's claim rested on the fact that chocolate contained carbohydrates and fats for energy, protein for building muscle and vitamins for health. But with the 'glass and a half' of full cream milk in every 1/2lb block of Cadbury's Dairy Milk suddenly impossible to come by, the iconic bar was shelved in 1941 to be replaced by the distinctly less luxurious-sounding Cadbury's Ration Bar, made with dried skimmed milk powder.

As the war went on, much of Cadbury's manufacturing based in the Midlands was co-opted for the war effort, under the umbrella of a new company called Bournville Utilities Limited. What had once been a factory where molten chocolate was moulded into bars, was adapted to make seats for Spitfires and five million gas masks. Other areas of the former chocolate factory were repurposed to produce rifles.

Cadbury's wasn't the only chocolate manufacturer contributing to the war effort. Bristol-based Fry would set up a mobile cocoa service, in a specially-equipped van, to serve hot chocolate to people who had been bombed out of their homes. Meanwhile, Terry's of York gave over their factory to make aeroplane propellers.

With sugar in increasingly short supply, the Ministry of Food had to make some more hard decisions that hit children particularly badly. On July 26th 1942, sweets were rationed.

To begin with, the new rules gave a sweet allowance of two ounces per week to every person over five years of age. That two ounces is roughly equivalent to the weight of a single Mars Bars. Fortunately, sweet rations were raised to four ounces per week shortly afterwards, but that's still only an average bag of Haribo in today's terms. Adults often gave up their rations for the children, with some particularly generous people leaving their sweetie coupons behind the counter at shops such as Woolworths. Some parents tried (mostly in vain) to persuade their sons and daughters to accept a carrot on a stick instead of a lolly.

Dark times for Britain's children indeed, when a carrot was considered an indulgence, as recalled by Yorkshire war baby Olga Gretton.

Olga Gretton, 92

I WAS BORN IN HULL in 1933. When I was six years old, two days before war was declared, I was evacuated. I knew nothing about what was going on. I was given a little rucksack with a packet of cream crackers in it, then I joined my schoolmates and we got on a train with no idea where we were going. My mother waved me off.

We were going to York. It took all day to go 40 miles. When we reached our destination we were taken to a school. I remember sitting in a baby chair with my gas mask round my neck. There were lots of adults about, taking children away with them. Just as I was thinking I would be left behind, a lovely lady came up and said, 'You're coming home with me.' This was the lady I'd come to know as Auntie Rose.

Auntie Rose took me and another little girl – Doreen Watton – back to her modern semi on the outskirts of the city. That teatime, she sat us down at a table in front of the French windows looking out into the garden. Suddenly, a man put his head round the edge of the window and grinned at us. This was Auntie Rose's husband, whom we'd call Uncle Harry. He was so excited to meet us girls, he couldn't wait to come inside to get a look at us. Rose and Harry were in their mid-twenties then, newly married, with no children of their own.

After a while, Doreen's mother came to fetch her and took her somewhere else but I stayed on and settled in. Every Friday afternoon, Auntie Rose took me into York to shop. We'd always go to Woolworths, where she'd buy me a little gift, like a red velvet-covered ball, which I treasured. After that we used to meet her sister Auntie Nora (everybody was 'auntie' in those days) and go for tea in Betty's famous café. Though they weren't able to serve the kind of luxurious cakes they'd served before the war, Betty's remained open throughout, even after it was hit by an incendiary bomb! The proprietor was very good at creating treats from salvaged goods.

Not long after I arrived in York, Uncle Harry was called up into the RAF and posted to Canada, leaving me and Auntie Rose alone. I remember each evening I would sit on her lap in the armchair for a cuddle. We didn't have much fruit in those days – oranges were reserved for the under-fives – so we used to eat raw carrots and pretend they were fruit instead.

Sweets were also in short supply. Before the war, Auntie Rose had worked in the Terry's chocolate factory, but most of the factory had been given over to the war effort. All the ladies in the family had worked at Terry's or at Rowntree's, York's other big confectioner, at some point. Sometimes, because we had those family connections, we would get the 'waste' misshapen chocs in addition to our rations but even then you were only allowed so many. The rest of the time we'd mix dried egg with sugar for a treat.

While Auntie Rose and I were cuddled up in the armchair, we'd sometimes listen to *Children's Hour*, but after that it was my bedtime. If I hadn't fallen asleep, at eight o'clock I would hear another show coming on downstairs: *The Man in Black*. The voice of the presenter would float up to my bedroom and I'd bury myself under the covers as he began, 'This is your storyteller, the man in black...' It was a horror drama series. I shouldn't have been listening but I couldn't help it. It scared me half to death.

I soon made friends with the children who lived on Auntie Rose's street and I went to the local school and the children I met there were very friendly too. I even got myself a little boyfriend. Auntie Rose was not at all pleased about that because he came from the wrong side of the tracks.

School was very strict in those days. You didn't mess around. I learned that the hard way. One morning it snowed but we were told we were not to go outside during playtime. I sneaked out with another child. When we came back in, we were given a good hiding with a 'battledore', which was a kind of wooden bat used for corporal punishment.

We hardly dared look at a teacher during classes. If there was something you didn't know, you were too frightened to say so. We could never do that. You were told to do things, not asked.

One afternoon a van turned up in the school playground and our teacher asked for volunteers to help the people in the van do some checks on our gas masks. I stuck my hand up but I soon wished I hadn't. I put my mask on and got into the van as instructed. While I was in there, someone whipped my mask off. They quickly put it back on again but in the brief time I didn't have it on, I took a couple of breaths and started choking.

I know now that it must have been one of the official 'gas vans' the government sent around to prepare the public for gas attacks. The vans were used to expose civilians – even small schoolchildren like me – to tear gas, to make sure we understood how to use our masks properly. It was a lesson I wouldn't forget.

My father wasn't called up because he worked in an exempt profession, at the Blackburn Aircraft Factory in Brough, near Hull, where they were making bombers and seaplanes for the Fleet Air Arm. My mother didn't work because my little sister was only three and a half and my parents had decided she was too young to be evacuated. Years later, I was told my mother had wanted to send me to Canada but my father wouldn't allow it.

My father died of tuberculosis in 1940. I had no idea when I left for York in September 1939 that I would never see him again. I remember Auntie Rose's mother, Grandma Holden, taking me on her knee and telling me my Daddy had died, but I was only seven and I don't think it really registered. I didn't go home for his funeral.

My dad's death meant my mother had to get a job to support me and my sister. She worked for a government department, collecting money from those families whose children had been evacuated to pay for their keep. She had to cycle all over the city in all weathers, which she believed later impacted her own health.

From time to time I would go home to see Mum for the weekend. Auntie Rose would put me on the train at York. She'd go along the carriages looking for a kind-looking lady to keep an eye on me until we got to Hull. At the end of the weekend, I did the same journey in reverse. Again, on my own. When I think about that now, I imagine my granddaughter, who's 19, as a six-year-old. I could never have let her go off on her own like that. How did the parents of evacuees do it? I suppose they knew they had to. Hull was being terribly bombed. It was an important port in those days.

York had been considered safe, but in 1942, it was bombed too, as part of the 'Baedeker Raids' Hitler ordered on Britain's most beautiful cities in an attempt to break the country's morale. They were called 'Baedeker Raids' after the German travel guides.

Each night, we had to go to one of the communal air raid shelters on the grass verge of our road. They were built of brick with a concrete roof. I don't know if they would have been much good if they got a direct hit. There was nothing much in the shelter, just a few benches. We would just sit there talking. Occasionally, we kids would lean out of our shelter and shout to the children in the shelters further down the street.

One night, we came out when the all clear sounded to find that lots of the houses on our street, including my friend's, had been set on fire by incendiary bombs. My friend was in the shelter with us at the time. Can you imagine coming out and seeing your home going up in flames?

We lived on Rawcliffe Avenue. A house on the adjacent street, Rawcliffe Lane, was completely destroyed and the people who lived there – including a little boy – were buried under the rubble in their shelter. They survived, thank goodness. Apparently, when the little boy was asked what it was like being buried, he responded, 'Oh, it was alright.' I imagine that's exactly what he said. We children were quite stoical. I don't remember feeling scared, despite all the destruction around us.

Around York there were a number of air stations where we'd see dozens of Lancaster bombers going out. After 1942, some of the stations were taken over by the Canadians and the American GIs. They used to put on parties for the evacuees and of course we all wanted to go because they could get sweets and chocolate and other things from their PX stores that we couldn't get hold of on our rations.

Because Mum was on her own, even when the Germans started bombing York, she decided it best I remain there. Eventually my little sister was old enough to be evacuated too. She came and stayed with Auntie Rose's sister, Auntie Nora. Though we weren't living together, we were at least with the same family and in those days everybody had get-togethers so we saw each other frequently.

My sister and I stayed on in York long after the war because Mum couldn't have us at home. As the war was ending, she got tuberculosis. She was sent to a sanitorium in Cottingham and stayed there for quite a while. In those days, they thought the cure for tuberculosis was fresh air so Mum had a room that was completely open to the elements on one side. We weren't allowed to visit in case we picked up TB ourselves. My sister and I had to go to a clinic every so often to be examined and drink cod liver oil to support our immunity. Cod liver oil was revolting but it did the job. I didn't ever catch the disease officially but I do have a TB scar on my lung, which shows up on X-rays.

When Mum eventually came out of the sanitorium, she looked nothing like I remembered. Through eating good food and not being allowed to do anything but rest, she had put on a lot of weight.

I didn't want to go back to Hull. That really upset Mum. But my sister and I had been happy in York. I think I was the luckiest evacuee ever, especially having heard the stories of the children who were treated like skivvies by their foster parents.

When we did eventually go home, I went back to York during every school holiday. I carried on going up there after I left school and started work too. Even after my mother remarried and we moved down to Wimbledon, I spent all my time off back in Yorkshire.

Eventually Auntie Rose and Uncle Harry had a child of their own, Barry. I stayed in touch with the whole family until Auntie Rose died in her 80s.

I do worry about the future. The First World War was supposed to be the war to end all wars, then we had World War Two and look what's going on in the world today. There's always a war somewhere. I can't get my head around it. We all die one day, why are we blasting people to pieces? It's the politicians, isn't it? Not the ordinary people, they don't want to go and fight another human being. It's politics and religion. And greed.

I think we've forgotten the lessons of World War Two because the people that experienced it are disappearing now. We're all dying off. And I despair, I despair! I think of all the ones that didn't come back: the young men that left wives or sweethearts at home, the children they never saw grow up, babies they never met. What a waste! And what about the Holocaust? What was it for? I look at my beautiful granddaughter and I get frightened for her and all the other young people.

I would advise the younger generations to be kind, have understanding for other people and try not to be manipulated by the internet. My generation has been lucky despite living through a war. We experienced the rebuilding of Britain. We've had 80 years of peace. We've been very, very lucky.

4

BLACK SATURDAY

The Blitz Begins

WHEN WAR WAS DECLARED IN September 1939, the people of Britain expected to face air raids and a German invasion within days, and indeed there were a couple of false alarms almost immediately. However, nothing much happened for the first few months. At least not on the home front. The period between September 1939 and the beginning of May 1940 was dubbed 'the Phoney War'.

Gradually, people began to relax and many of the parents who had been so eager to see their children evacuated began to wonder whether they had overreacted; particularly those parents whose children seemed unhappy in their foster homes and those who were reaching an age – 14 – when they might be able to help family finances by leaving school and getting a job. One by one, evacuees were quietly being brought back home.

This was troubling for the government and the late spring of 1940 saw another propaganda push to persuade parents that their children really were better off left in their foster homes, far from Hitler's attention. A notice placed by the London County Council in the *Daily Express* in May 1940 warned parents, 'should they not take the opportunity which the Government offers for the evacuation of schoolchildren from London, they will be incurring *a grave responsibility.'*

The war was only just getting started. On May 10th 1940, the Germans invaded Belgium, the Netherlands and France. In a matter of days, the British Expeditionary Force, which had been fighting with the Belgians and the French, was driven to the northwest coast of France, leaving escape across the Channel the only option.

The evacuation of Dunkirk is one of the best-known stories of World War Two. The operation, codenamed Dynamo, was headed up by Admiral Bertram Ramsay, who had been called out of retirement in 1939.

The operation involved some 800 naval vessels but the nature of the beach at Dunkirk meant that many of the bigger ships could not get close enough to the shore to pick up passengers. For this reason, the Admiralty had to appeal to the civilian owners of small boats harboured along the south coast of the UK to lend a hand. In the end, these 'little ships' helped to evacuate 338,000 members of the BEF and the French troops who had been fighting alongside them.

The success of the 'little ships' provided a great morale boost for the British public but in truth the situation in France was a disaster. Though hundreds of thousands had been rescued, more than 90,000 Allied troops had to be left behind, along with much valuable equipment. Britain would need its 'Dunkirk Spirit' more than ever over the coming months.

France fell to the Germans. Shortly after that, the Channel Islands were invaded, bringing the German occupation to the British Isles. In July 1940, the Battle of Britain began, with dog fights between the RAF and the Luftwaffe in the sky over south-east England. Then on September 7th 1940 – a day that would become known as Black Saturday – around 350 enemy bombers, accompanied by more than 600 fighter planes, made their way to London to unleash the Blitz on ordinary British families such as that of six-year-old Dorrie Clowry...

Dot Clowry, 91

WHEN THE WAR BEGAN WE were living in Southfields, London. I was five years old. I had two younger brothers, Bob and James, whom we called Jim. There were just three and a half years between the three of us. When they were small, my brothers couldn't say my name, so they called me 'Dodo'. Mum and Dad called me 'Dorrie'.

With Dad away in the army, it must have been hard for Mum to cope with three small children. She certainly wouldn't have wanted to try to get us all out of the house and into the shelter if an air raid happened in the night.

We had an Anderson shelter in the back garden, partially buried in the ground and covered in concrete. You had to go down some steps to get into it. There were bunkbeds inside but the only light came from candles. It wasn't very luxurious but every evening Mum would dress us in our pyjamas and take us down to the shelter to sleep, so she didn't have to worry if the siren went. This was our routine in the early autumn of 1940, when a German bomber dropped a high explosive bomb that wiped out half our street.

We didn't know exactly what had happened because when the bomb exploded, it blew debris all over our shelter, burying us underneath tonnes of rubble. When the all clear sounded, we found we couldn't get out. The door to the shelter was wedged shut. All we could do was wait: me, Mum and my two little brothers, in the blackest dark I have ever known. Once our candles had burned out, there was not a flicker of light. Not a glimmer. We could not see a thing. Not a thing. It's how I imagine it must be to be blind.

In the cold, pitch black we sat and we waited, listening for the rescuers outside. I don't know how long it took them to find us but it felt like forever. Sometimes we could hear voices nearby but they never seemed to get to us. We must have shouted when they got close but I suppose there were injured people outside on the street to be dealt with first. Perhaps they didn't hear us and thought we were already dead. As she did her best to keep me and my little brothers distracted, I don't know how Mum kept it together. She must have been as frightened as we were. It was like being buried alive.

When at last the rescuers got to us and the door to the shelter opened, we ran out into the light. The first thing we saw was that four or five houses to one side of ours had been flattened. Our own house wasn't completely gone like the others but one wall had fallen away, so that we could see our staircase, open to the elements, like we were looking into a dolls' house.

We couldn't go back inside, of course, so we had to go to stay with our maternal grandmother, Nan. Because he'd heard our street had been hit, Mum's brother – my uncle – had already come to find us on his bicycle. While Mum carried what little we'd had with us in the shelter, my uncle balanced my two brothers on his bike – Bob on the saddle and Jim on the crossbar – and pushed them all the way to Nan's house while I walked alongside. I was still dressed in my nightclothes and wearing my slippers. All my other clothes and my proper shoes were in the house. It was too dangerous to try to retrieve them.

It just so happened that the day after we were bombed out, Dad came home from the army on leave. He didn't have a clue what had been going on. When he got to the end of our street, he found a police blockade, preventing him from going any further. Seeing the bomb damage, he panicked. He tried to tell the police that his family home was behind their blockade but they told him, 'You can't go down there.'

'Watch me,' Dad said and he vaulted over the barrier and ran straight past them. I don't suppose they tried to stop him after that. I mean, who wouldn't break the rules if they thought their children had been caught up in a bomb?

When Dad got to what remained of our house, he was greeted by some neighbours, who were still living on the undamaged side of the street. They told him what had happened and assured him we were all safe. He came to find us at Nan's and contacted his superiors in the army, who let him have a few days of compassionate leave.

There was no way we'd be able to move back to the house any time soon – in fact we never did – but my parents and two uncles went back a few days after the bombing to try to salvage some of our belongings. In the scullery, which was more or less intact, my uncles found the washing my mother had left soaking in the stone 'copper' as we called the basin. They stood there wringing it out so that they could bring it back to Nan's.

Among the other things Mum rescued was my favourite baby doll, which was made of papier mache. Her head was all squashed. Mum wrapped the doll up and put it in the bottom drawer of Nan's wardrobe for a crib.

We were at my nan's for about three months, I think. She looked after us while Mum went to work at a children's clothing factory on Wandsworth High Street, where my aunt was the manager. My aunt did ARP work in the evenings, checking people were obeying the blackout rules. Each evening, as it started to get dark, we had to make sure the curtains were properly drawn so that no chink of light could be seen from outside. All Nan's window panes were covered with brown paper to stop glass coming into the room if they were blown out.

Despite what had happened to us in the shelter, Mum was determined that she wouldn't let us be evacuated. Several times the authorities came round to try to persuade her it would be the best thing for me and my brothers, but she always refused. Lots of children from the area were being evacuated. We would see them being loaded onto buses and I was always very glad I wasn't going with them. I was even more glad that Mum stood her ground when I heard about the way some of the evacuees were treated, used as slave labour and worse by the strangers who took them home.

We were much happier staying in London with Mum and our nan. Nan was a lovely woman – only five feet tall with a mass of pure white hair. We loved her to bits. Her house had a long garden, in which she grew all sorts of fruit and vegetables. There was an Anderson shelter too. Surprisingly, given what had happened before, I didn't mind going down there. When we had to go into the shelter, Nan would keep us distracted. She taught me all sorts of things during the air raids – like how to recite the alphabet backwards and lots of songs.

Nan introduced us to some new food too, thanks to her vegetable garden. She loved lettuce. One of her favourite things was to make a white bread sandwich with a filling of lettuce leaves, sprinkled with sugar. She called them 'buppa sugar sandwiches' and she would eat them with great delight, declaring, 'Oooh these are lovely,' which made us want to try them too.

I remember Mum asking me and my brothers whether we wanted to have sugar in our tea or save our sugar rations to make some sweets. We chose the sweets, so she and my aunt made toffee from scratch, boiling the sugar in water until it started to cara-melise. My brothers and I would watch as they stood at either end of the kitchen table stretching the toffee out between them and laughing all the while. When the toffee was set, they'd chop it up into sections – some was sent to Dad in the army, the rest was for us. It was very sticky and probably terrible for our teeth but it was absolutely delicious. You can't get anything that tastes nearly so good in the shops.

Everything was on the ration, not just food, so we were careful with what we had. We didn't get much coal so at the end of the night, Nan would use potato peelings to 'bank up' the fire so that it was still alight when we woke up in the morning. She used the ash as fertiliser in the garden. She was thrifty in so many ways. She even used soap flakes meant for washing clothes on her hair. Perhaps that's why her hair was so white!

All through the war I went to school at St Michael's on Granville Road. One of the things we had to do at school was practice putting on our gas masks. I hated that. I hated the horrible smell of rubber. In the evenings, we would listen to the wireless – music and the news etc – and there would often be public information announcements intoning, 'Have you got your gas mask?' which frightened me half to death. I dreaded hearing the rattle that warned of a gas attack.

We had to carry our gas masks everywhere but in general we had a lot of freedom. Mum would just open the door and tell us to go out and play. We made our own entertainment. We'd play hopscotch and skipping games. We climbed all over the bombsites. We got used to seeing freshly bombed houses with beds and other bits of furniture hanging out of them. Because where we lived was at the centre of a triangle formed by three railway stations, the Germans were dropping bombs near us all the time.

During Dad's second leave from the army, he came back to London to help Mum find us a new place to live. Because so many people had chosen to be evacuated, there were plenty of empty houses. Dad found an upstairs flat in a house on Camborne Road. When we moved in, I don't suppose he and Mum had any idea they would be there for the next 50 years. Eventually, they had the whole house.

Not long after we moved, the Germans dropped a bomb at the end of that road too. There was nothing like the damage we'd seen at our old house but all the windows in our flat were blown out and we had to move back to Nan's while we waited for them to be replaced.

Dad was an army cook. He was sent on a training course with Lyons, the caterers, and ended up cooking for the soldiers at an army camp in Billingshurst. The camp was next to a farm and Dad became friendly with a farm labourer and his wife. He'd take them tins of supplies from the camp which he would swap for fresh ingredients like eggs and bacon that were very popular with the soldiers.

Dad became so friendly with the farm labourer and his wife that they invited us to stay with them during the school holidays. They were very kind to us. The wife of the couple told Mum that she could 'do whatever she wanted', so it felt like a home away from home. We loved the freedom of the fields and seeing the shire horses that pulled some of the farm machinery.

We were usually on the farm at harvest time. The farm hands would cut the fields of corn by driving the tractor round and round in a decreasing spiral to the middle. In doing this, they frightened the wild rabbits, who would run to the middle to escape the noise. Unfortunately for the poor rabbits, we would be ready for them. The local adults would catch dozens in one go, which we would help to skin for the pot.

Later in the war, two German POWs were brought to work on the farm. They were very young lads, no more than 18. I remember one of them was called Paul. These German lads were both very friendly and used to help us up onto the backs of the Shire horses then lead us around the yard so we could learn to ride.

One day, while we were on the farm, playing near the shire horses, my brother Jim had a little accident. While one of the men was throwing a harness over one of the horses, a loose buckle caught Jim on the side of the neck. When a lump came up a few days later, everyone assumed it was where the buckle had hit him, but when Mum took him to the doctor, it was discovered that he had TB. He'd probably caught it from the unpasteurised milk we drank when we stayed on the farm.

Poor Jim had to spend a year in a sanitorium, where the patients had to sleep in beds pushed outside onto the verandah for the fresh air. My other brother and I weren't allowed to visit but Mum went to see him whenever she could. Unfortunately, that wasn't very often because she had no money for the train ticket.

You had to pay to see a doctor in those days so people relied on a lot of home remedies. Mum made a concoction with brown sugar and thinly sliced onion, which she would layer in a jar. Over time the juice from the onions would mix with the sugar to make a syrup that could be used as cough mixture. When I had croup, it was very good for that. When I had chilblains, she would take a slice of the onion and bandage it against the affected toes. It seemed to work. It doesn't sound very nice but I came to love the taste of onions. I still love them now.

At the end of the war, we had a street party. Mum made me a red, white and blue dress. We were very lucky that Mum was an excellent seamstress. All through the war, when we couldn't get new clothes because they were rationed, she would make sure my dresses still fitted by adding in extra panels made from old bed sheets. She would chop the bottom few inches off the hem and stitch in a panel before adding the hem back on so that it looked as if it was meant to be that way. People always thought I had a brand new clothes.

So, I had a red, white and blue dress for the VE day party. The adults set up trestle tables all the way down the street and everybody contributed food. The tables were groaning with sandwiches and cakes. People had been saving ingredients from their rations for weeks – ever since it looked like the war might be finishing – so that we could have this one big blow-out.

Towards the end of the war, Dad became an army tank trailer driver, a role which took him to France and across to Germany. He was part of a three-man team. When they found an abandoned tank – Allied or German – they would load it on the back of the trailer to be taken to be repaired or broken down for parts. If they came across a German tank, they would inevitably find a dead soldier or two still inside.

Dad wasn't part of the troops that liberated Belsen but he did meet some of that concentration camp's former inmates when he got to Germany. He said that he'd never been so shocked by anything before. The state those poor people were in was horrific.

Because of the things he'd seen, Dad believed in what he had been fighting for and for years after – his whole life, in fact – whenever he heard the National Anthem, he would stand to attention. My brothers and I would sometimes laugh at him but Mum would always tell us off for that. She understood. Dad was very patriotic, a soldier through and through.

Perhaps it's the case that my mind has blocked the bad parts out but apart from the night we first got bombed out, the war years were quite a happy time for me. That said, I know that being buried in that shelter did affect me. I've had claustrophobia ever since.

For a long time afterwards, I would wake up in the night, panting and panicking and shouting, 'I can't breathe, I can't breathe!' until Mum came in and put on the light. I still like to have it light at night time. That's why I like living in London. With the street lamps and all the other houses around me, it's never really dark in the city.

Another thing is that I cannot lay on my back. Not when I'm sleeping or awake. When I had a cataract operation, I had to tell the consultant that I wouldn't be able to lay down on the operating table. He had to operate on me while I was sitting up. It's the same with the dentist. I just can't lay flat. It takes me back to being on my bunk bed in the shelter. But in general, when I do think back to those days, I remember the good times more than the bad.

5

THE LUFTWAFFE COMES TO HARROGATE

'There came the loudest crump of all and the dining-room window blew in'

THE FIRST NIGHT OF THE Blitz, Black Saturday, left more than 400 Londoners dead and many, many more with terrible injuries. The Luftwaffe's *Unternehmen Loge* (Loge was the German code-name for London) would continue for eight long months. At the same time, the Germans targeted other strategic military positions outside the capital.

The elegant North Yorkshire spa town of Harrogate had been transformed by the war. On the town's famous strip of public parkland, The Stray, trenches were dug to prevent German planes from landing. Other parts of the Stray (so called because the public could graze animals there without tether) had been planted with vegetables. In addition, many service personnel were stationed in or around Harrogate. The No 7 Personnel Reception Centre, which served as a processing facility for RAF aircrew awaiting postings, was based in the town. Several of the town's hotels had been requisitioned to serve as temporary accommodation for the aircrew and as administrative offices for the Air Ministry. There was also a

Women's Auxiliary Air Force training centre and an Air Ministry medical training establishment. At HMS Forest Moor, a Royal Navy land base and 'Y' station in the Harrogate borough of Nidderdale, officers listened in to enemy radio signals. Meanwhile, nearby Newby Hall was earmarked as a potential refuge by the Coats Mission, a British army unit with responsibility for evacuating the Royal Family in the event of an emergency. There were plenty of reasons for the Luftwaffe to target Harrogate. And it did.

At around lunchtime on September 12th 1940, Harrogate was visited by a single Luftwaffe bomber, which dropped its load over the town's Majestic Hotel, believing it to be a British military headquarters. The mission was ultimately unsuccessful but it was a seminal moment in the life of war baby Ann Hay, whose family lived in the house right across the road.

Ann Hay, 88

AT THE OUTSET OF WAR my family moved from Croydon to Harrogate, as my father, who was in a protected job with the Air Ministry, was transferred to York. My parents took a lease on a house in Springfield Avenue but almost as soon as we were settled in my father was sent back to London. My mother and I stayed put and my brother was born in Yorkshire in November 1939.

Very soon after my brother arrived, there was an air-raid warning and we were told to leave our homes and find a shelter. My mother knew next to nobody in Harrogate at that time. She was alone with a little girl (me), a very young baby, a Sealyham dog and a tabby cat. The only person she did know was Mr Ward, the removals man, who had brought our furniture up from Croydon. She telephoned him to ask for advice, and he fetched us to his house for the night. My mother and I shared a single spare bed and my baby brother slept in the bottom drawer of a chest. We were allowed home the following day.

The house we lived in was the right-hand half of a late-Victorian building. The previous inhabitants were a doctor and his wife. On the ground floor, on the right as you looked at it, was our dining room, with a bow window with stained glass inset, which had been the doctor's consulting room. At the far end of the hall was the kitchen, with a Rayburn stove and a marvellous cabinet called an Easiwork, which was as close as you got to a fitted kitchen in those days.

Two small rooms led off the kitchen, a pantry where all the crockery, tins and packets lived. Then on the other side, the scullery, where all the wet jobs were done. We had a big ceramic jar full of watery liquid for preserving eggs. Whenever we got surplus eggs I had to write the date on the shell with a pencil that turned your tongue purple when you licked it. Another big jar had salt water in, into which we put runner beans and other vegetables to preserve them. You had to wash them well to get rid of the salt but they stayed fit to eat for ages.

A door in the passage led to the cellars, one of which was full of coal, which was delivered down a chute from a manhole-cover in the pavement outside. The other cellar was set up to be used as an air raid shelter. It was a bit spidery in there.

At the top of the house, were the servants' rooms. These were not in use, but in the second year of the war we had a refugee family called the Bernays come to lodge with us, with their grown-up daughter Mara. I never knew what nationality they were.

The garden was mostly grass, though I did have a playhouse. Much of my playtime was spent in the garden of the Majestic Hotel, which was opposite our house.

There was a big RAF station near York and from the beginning I was devoted to the airmen. There were night flights over our house and after I had been put to bed I would get up and sit on the window sill and watch the bombers go overhead – I can still remember the sound – and I would wake early each morning to hear them come back and hope my friends were safe.

We quickly got used to the blackout. When we went out after dark there were no street lights and we had to use torches with strips of black tape criss-crossing the glass to cut down the light. We had a car, and it had taped headlights so only a cross of about 1cm width was revealed, giving very little light. However there was very little petrol so we could not often use it.

So many things were rationed. I remember the sweet ration particularly. We had 1/4lb a week. Dolly Mixture was very popular as it felt as though we were getting more. Nothing came wrapped; it was all in big glass jars and weighed out from brass scoops into white paper bags. Chocolate was wrapped and I believed that the reason for the 1/4lb bar having eight squares was so we could eat one square a day and two on Sundays.

I remember that bananas arrived by ship – once – one banana per child, and the relatives crowded round to watch my brother and me eat ours. I'd never heard of bananas and didn't even know you had to peel them. I didn't like it very much. With hindsight I expect they were shipped over under ripe, but everyone said how lucky we were the banana ship had safely got through in the convoy.

At school we had a gas mask drill each day. I kept mine in a silver-coloured case with Mickey Mouse on it. We had to put our masks on and make cow-noises. We mooed as loudly as we could. The theory was if the teacher could hear us then the mask didn't fit properly. My poor brother, being a baby, was too small for a gas mask. He had to be put in a respirator, a rubberised canvas container with a Perspex window and a charcoal filter. By the time he was ten he had awful asthma and I think this early experience could have been responsible.

We listened to the wireless a lot. We had a big set in the drawing room, and a portable, which was huge by today's standards, powered by a car battery, which we took down to the cellar during air-raids. The news broadcasts were very important. Newsreaders started giving their names, so listeners would know what they were hearing was a genuine news bulletin and not the Germans. They would start, 'Here is the six o'clock news and this is Alvar Liddell reading it', or John Snagge – these are the two I remember best. Every midday there was a programme called *Music While You Work* which was broadcast from various factories doing war-work, also *Workers' Playtime* which included comedy turns.

My favourite comedy shows were Richard Murdoch and Kenneth Horne in 'Much-Binding-in-the-Marsh' which took place on a supposed RAF station in the wilds of nowhere, all about current issues of the war as a send-up. The army had a similar spoof in Charlie Chester's *Stand Easy*. Max Wall had a show called *Our Shed*, which was about local yokels.

Much of my knowledge of the war's progress came from Giles' cartoons in the *Daily Express*, and I really believed that Mussolini and Goebbels looked as they did in the drawings...

Then came the raid on us. Just as we were sitting down to eat the siren gave its eerie whooping call.

My mother ordered me to the cellar at once, following me down the steps with my baby brother. Aunt Minna, who was staying with us, grabbed a bowl of stew from the stove and some spoons, then came down too, shutting the door behind her. There were bunk beds and a table, and a single light bulb on a long cord. I was pushed on to a lower bunk, while my baby brother, well-wrapped, was tucked into a wooden crate labelled Moët et Chandon.

The grown-ups sat on the bunk opposite, finishing the stew before lying down to rest. Heavy thuds seemed to shake the building, and the light-bulb swung on its cord, casting worrying shadows.

I was still hungry, remembering a dish of stewed apple that had been left on the dining-room table. When the adults seemed to be asleep. I slid from my bunk, then sneaked up the steps into the dining-room. There on the table stood the brown baking-dish. I seized it, holding its lukewarmness to my chest, when there came the loudest crump of all and the dining-room window blew in.

Across the floor lay a river of shining glass fragments, up to and around my sandalled feet. Too startled to scream, I just stood there, clutching the dish. I heard my mother calling my name; she came running in, stopping in the doorway of the devastated dining-room, then crunched her way towards me. She took the dish from me, and when I protested she said gently, 'It's got glass in it, Ann dear. We can't eat it.'

Later the ARP wardens came round to all the houses in the Avenue. An unexploded bomb had gone down the lift-shaft of the Majestic Hotel and we must all get clear till the Bomb Disposal Squad had made it safe.

Mercifully my brother's pram had not been in its usual place in the dining-room or it would have been full of glass. My mother loaded him into it and put our Sealyham Jilly on her lead. The adults had had their coats with them in the cellar, ready to go, but my coat was upstairs and there was no time to fetch it, so a grey blanket was thrown round my pyjamas – hand-me-downs from the boys next door – and we were bustled out. I worried about our cat Tigger, but was assured cats were survivors and he'd have hidden away somewhere safe. We joined the area's other motley refugees and trekked up to the Cairncross Hotel, a safe distance, where we were put in the public rooms, with chairs if you were lucky, otherwise sitting on the floor while the staff reluctantly provided us with cups of tea.

Eventually, we were allowed back home, and the task of clearing up and repairing could begin. To my joy, Tigger reappeared from wherever his secret hiding-place had been. The Majestic was closed till the hole in the roof was fixed. My friend, who lived there, came over to tell me of the excitement of his night. The lift, of course, was totally wrecked, and the vibration had knocked down most of the chandeliers. There was a lot of mess. My friend made it sound more exciting than my little adventure, though I felt I'd had enough drama and vowed I would never eat stewed apple again lest it might have glass in it.

On the lunch-time news nearly five years later, a recording of church bells rang out, and Alvar Liddell the newsreader announced that Mr Churchill was to speak. The war in Europe was over! Not yet in the Far East, but we had beaten Germany at last. VE Day was to be celebrated on May 8th, with street-parties nationwide. The bells began to ring from our own church; I didn't remember ever having heard them before.

Harrogate was to have a big party on The Stray, the public park, and my mother said she'd take me. It was a historic happening, she said – she was a great one for these occasions and had told me that, when I was a baby, she and my father had taken me to watch the Crystal Palace burn down, so I could tell my children.

It was a mild evening. We took the black sticky-tape off our torches so we could use the whole beam. I flashed mine about, delighted not to hear the angry roar of, 'Put that light out!' The street lamps were on, and people had left their curtains open, so we could see from the top of the bus inside their rooms. The bus was free that night, because of The Occasion.

On The Stray were what seemed like millions of people, waving torches and flags, dancing and singing, 'Run Rabbit', 'Tipperary', 'Bluebirds' and others, very loudly. My mother was dancing and singing too. I was terrified of losing her, and clung on to the belt of her Burberry. My calm, unflappable mother, coping with two young children, fire-watching as an ARP warden, running the house while my father was in London throughout the Blitz, and I know she was scared for him; I'd seen her crying over his letters sometimes. Yet here she was, behaving as madly as everyone else.

The noise grew louder, people were hugging, kissing each other. Some hugged my mother, some even tried to kiss me! I just wanted to go home, away from all these excited crowds. To my shame I started crying. Someone pointed this out to my mother, who realised I was scared and agreed to leave.

We struggled through the crowds, but were unable to find a bus. A kind RAF officer with a motorbike, who was staying at the Majestic, packed us into his sidecar and took us home. I ran straight up to my room and dived under the bedclothes, fully dressed. My mother explained I was just over-excited. But from that day to this I have always hated and feared crowds and group emotion. VE Day had bitten deep.

A few months later Japan surrendered. The war was over. We could move back south again. My father was still working with his Ministry in London, but he and my mother did not want to live there. They found a big old house in a country town about 30 miles away from Harrogate and that's where we stayed.

More than 80 years later, I still don't like stewed apple.

6

'SEAVACUEES' AND THE SS CITY OF BENARES

OPERATION PIED PIPER WAS INTENDED to put children out of harm's way but for some the move from Britain's beleaguered cities was a case of 'out of the frying pan and into the fire'. While many children found themselves in loving foster homes, with people who were determined to treat their young houseguests as part of the family, others were less lucky. Some found themselves used as unpaid labour. And, as was discovered in 1940, when Hitler unleashed his Blitzkrieg, many safe havens were no longer as secure as everyone had thought.

The only way safety could be guaranteed was by putting children far out of the range of the Luftwaffe and the Kriegsmarine. To that effect, since the beginning of the war, several wealthy British families had controversially sent their children to stay with relatives overseas.

Evacuation outside the UK was an expensive business, a dream solution far out of the reach of the poor families of London's East End or Manchester or Liverpool. A variety of MPs, including the Labour leader Clement Atlee, didn't think this was fair. Thanks to their lobbying, a government sponsored scheme known as the Children's Overseas Reception Scheme, overseen by the Children's

Overseas Reception Board (CORB), was born. CORB would send children from all sections of British society to Australia, New Zealand, South Africa, Canada and the United States. Its services were to be made available to every British family.

It seemed a perfect solution but there were several high-profile people who were still not keen on sending any British children overseas, believing that such evacuations helped only the enemy and damaged morale at home. Winston Churchill was not a fan. Neither was Queen Elizabeth, wife of King George VI.

At the beginning of the war, it had been suggested that the Queen and her daughters, the Princesses Elizabeth and Margaret, be sent to Canada or North America until such time as their safety in the United Kingdom could be guaranteed. The King's second cousin, Lord Mountbatten had already sent his two daughters to New York. The Queen responded in a letter, which soon became famous. On Windsor Castle headed notepaper, she wrote, 'The children will not leave unless I do. I shall not leave unless their father does, and the King will not leave the country in any circumstances, whatever.'

The Queen's letter sent a clear signal that the British Royal Family – even its youngest members - would stand alongside its citizens through thick and thin. There was to be no running away.

All the same, CORB might have evacuated hundreds of thousands of children. When it was announced that applications could be made through schools, the scheme proved to be incredibly popular, with anxious parents signing up more than 210,000 of their sons and daughters. The task ahead was enormous. More than 1,000 suitable volunteer escorts had to be found for the first phase of the scheme which would evacuate 24,000.

To expedite evacuations, the embarkation process was streamlined. In the days prior to departure, the 'seavacuees' stayed in hostels, where they could be given the medical checks required by the host nations to which they were travelling. Some bureaucracy was dispensed with altogether. The children did not need passports but were instead given identity discs which carried their CORB number.

The CORB evacuation ships would join Allied convoys for the dangerous passage through the eastern Atlantic, where the German navy's U-boats hunted in 'wolf packs'. As the date of the first CORB 'seavacuations' approached, everything seemed to be going well.

One of the first CORB ships to leave was the SS Volendam, borrowed from the Holland America Line. On August 29th 1940, the Volendam joined a convoy leaving Liverpool, bound for Halifax and New York. Also in the convoy was the RMS Rangitata, with a cargo of evacuees bound for New Zealand.

Only one day into her voyage, SS Volendam was torpedoed but, by some miracle, she didn't sink. There was only one casualty, the ship's purser, who drowned. All the children were rescued and the ship was towed to Scotland to be repaired. It was only once Volendam was safely in dock that it was discovered she had actually been hit by a second torpedo, which was still embedded in her bow. If that second torpedo had exploded, the ship likely would not have survived.

Almost all of the 321 children who had been onboard the Volendam returned to their anxious families in Britain rather than continue on their way to Canada and the US. One can only imagine how hard it would have been to send those children off again, after such a stark reminder of the danger they might face while Hitler's wolf packs prowled the waves. The news of the Volendam's close call with the Kriegsmarine must have been in the minds of the parents whose children were scheduled to sail on the SS City of Benares.

The City of Benares was a steam turbine ocean liner. She was relatively new, only finished in 1936. When war was declared, City of Benares was sent to Cape Town in South Africa, where she was prepared to sail in wartime. She was painted with grey camouflage to disguise her from U Boats and fitted with a gun on her stern deck.

In May 1940, City of Benares' owner, Ellerman Lines, offered the ship and two of her sister ships for CORB duties. Her first voyage, to Montreal, was scheduled to depart Liverpool on Friday September 13th that same year.

Captained by Captain Landles Nicoll, City of Benares was carrying 408 people when she joined Convoy OB213 that fateful Friday. Her passengers included 90 CORB children, aged between five and 15, and their ten escorts. City of Benares was put in the centre column of the convoy, protected by two Royal Navy corvettes, HMS Gloxinia and HMS Gladiolus, and a destroyer, HMS Winchelsea.

Among the CORB children on board were 12-year-old Patricia Allen and ten-year-old Michael Brooker, who had both survived the U-boat attack on the Volendam. Having been rescued from the Volendam, Patricia had returned to Liverpool, only to discover that her family home had been destroyed in an air raid. Michael Brooker was unable to return to his home because it now contained an unexploded bomb.

The Grimmond family of Brixton had also been bombed out of their house. It was for that reason Mr and Mrs Edward Grimmond had decided they would sign up five of their 11 children to the CORB scheme. The Grimmond children were put on the reserve list for a sailing but were added to the passengers scheduled to sail on the City of Benares after CORB volunteers heard what a terrible time they'd had in the Blitz and decided they deserved to jump the queue.

The Grimmond children, Patricia Allen, and Michael Brooker were not the only passengers who had already had close brushes with death before they arrived in Liverpool. Among the adults sailing that day was German baroness Mrs Amelie von Ingersleben, a writer, critical of Hitler's Reich, who had escaped from a concentration camp.

Shortly after City of Benares left Liverpool, a German reconnaissance plane was spotted overhead. This was not good news, suggesting the convoy would soon be firmly in the Kriegsmarine's sights. The CORB children joined the rest of the passengers on the deck for lifeboat drills. They were instructed to sleep in their lifejackets. Just in case.

It was during the evening of September 17th that the City of Benares was sighted by German submarine U-48. The U-boat fired two torpedoes at the ship at 10pm. Both those torpedoes missed their target, but a minute later, a third torpedo struck.

Within 15 minutes, the captain had ordered that the ship be abandoned, but the crew had trouble lowering the lifeboats. Within half an hour, City of Benares was sunk and only one out of the 12 lifeboats she carried had been successfully launched. At the time that City of Benares was hit, she was more than 600 miles from the closest inhabited land.

It took 24 hours for HMS Hurricane to reach the site of City of Benares' sinking. They were able to pick up 105 survivors, including seven of the CORB children – three girls and four boys. HMS Hurricane did not find Lifeboat 12 that day and it was assumed that she had been lost to the waves.

Lifeboat 12 was adrift for eight long days before she was sighted by an RAF Short Sunderland, which alerted convoy escort HMS Anthony. Among the people onboard were six CORB evacuees and their escorts Father Rory O'Sullivan and Mary Cornish.

On September 19th, Geoffrey Shakespeare, Director General of CORB, had written to the parents of the children who were lost, presumed dead. In his letter to Tom Myatt, now kept in the archives at the Imperial War Museum, he expressed his condolences upon the loss of Mr Myatt's daughter Beryl, saying, 'Like so many other parents you were anxious to send your child overseas to one of the Dominions to enjoy a happier and safer life. You courageously took this decision in the interest of your child, believing that this course was better than leaving the child here in a vulnerable area subject to continuous air raids. Mr Shakespeare concluded, 'Unhappily the course of war has shown that neither by land nor sea can there be complete safety.'

Of the 90 CORB children who boarded City of Benares in Liverpool, 77 did not come home. One was killed in the explosion, the others died in the sinking or of exposure on lifeboats. Patricia Allen, Michael Brooker and the Grimmond children – Augusta, Constance, Edward, Leonard and Violet – were among the lost.

When news of the sinking of the City of Benares reached the general public, there was outrage. There were strict rules of engagement when it came to refugee ships and Germany had breached them. The Germans' response was to blame the British government for sending children on ships through a war zone after repeated warnings. To the Germans, the City of Benares was a legitimate target. It was claimed that certain passengers were heading to America with the intention of persuading the United States to enter the conflict. Furthermore, the ship would be used to bring war supplies back to Britain on her return.

That the SS Volendam had been torpedoed two weeks earlier had already started to sway public opinion regarding the sense of CORB's noble scheme. After the sinking of City of Benares, public support plummeted and Churchill, who had been opposed to the scheme from the start, hastened its cancellation.

All those children who had been selected for the scheme – some of whom were already onboard ships waiting to sail – were sent home. While private evacuations saw a further 14,000 children sent overseas, the government's involvement in such a project was over.

After the war, Heinrich Bleichrodt, the captain of the U-boat which sunk City of Benares, was tried for war crimes. He continued to deny that he had any knowledge that the ship was carrying evacuees and insisted that his decision to torpedo City of Benares was legitimate. He was backed up by members of his crew, who reaffirmed that they had no way of knowing who was onboard. While he was officially unrepentant, reports from his crew suggested that, privately, Bleichrodt never got over hearing that he had unwittingly targeted a ship full of children.

7

PRINCESS ELIZABETH'S FIRST SPEECH

'Goodnight and good luck to you all.'

BY NOW THE PHONEY WAR was well and truly over. On September 13th 1940, Buckingham Palace was hit by five high explosive bombs, leading the Queen to declare, 'I am glad we have been bombed. Now we can look the East End in the eye.'

With the Blitz raging and the sinking of the City Of Benares in the news, it seemed the children of Britain had never been more in danger. They were badly in need of a morale boost and it was decided that the most famous children in the United Kingdom would be the ones to deliver it.

On October 13th 1940, a month after the bombing of Buckingham Palace, young Princess Elizabeth – then just 14 years old – took to the airwaves to give her very first public speech. She spoke during *Children's Hour*, the popular radio programme beloved of so many children throughout the British Empire. From a makeshift studio in a drawing room at Windsor Castle, she told her listeners, 'In wishing you all "good evening" I feel that I am speaking to friends and companions who have shared with my sister and myself many a happy *Children's Hour*.'

The young Princess directly addressed the evacuees, 'Thousands of you in this country have had to leave your homes and be separated from your fathers and mothers. My sister Margaret Rose and I feel so much for you as we know from experience what it means to be away from those we love most of all.

'To you, living in new surroundings, we send a message of true sympathy and at the same time we would like to thank the kind people who have welcomed you to their homes in the country.'

The Princess then went on to address those children who had been evacuated overseas, telling her listeners that she felt able to imagine the sort of lives they were leading from having talked to her parents about their Royal visits to the far-flung reaches of the Commonwealth. She promised the seavacuees that they were not forgotten. The Princess ended her speech on a note of optimism.

'We know, every one of us, that in the end all will be well; for God will care for us and give us victory and peace. And when peace comes, remember it will be for us, the children of today, to make the world of tomorrow a better and happier place.'

Princess Margaret then joined her big sister at the microphone to say goodnight before Princess Elizabeth brought the broadcast to a close with the words that everyone would remember, 'Goodnight, and good luck to you all.'

Throughout the war, Princess Elizabeth and her younger sister made an important public contribution to the war effort. Photographs of the princesses participating in wartime activities were widely published in newspapers and magazines. They were photographed knitting for the forces and working on the allotments at Windsor Castle in support of the Dig For Victory campaign.

The Royal Household had its own charity – the Royal Household Wool Fund – which supplied yarn for military clothing, and each Christmas between 1940 and 1944, the princesses took part in a pantomime, alongside children from the Royal Windsor School and the local community, to raise money for the fund's endeavours. The pantomimes were performed in the castle's Waterloo Chamber, and were watched by audiences of up to 600 people, including the King and Queen.

Princess Elizabeth would often take the traditional pantomime role of 'principal boy'. She played the Prince in *Sleeping Beauty* and *Cinderella*. In 1943, she took the starring role in a production of *Aladdin*. Music was provided by the Grenadier Guards. The princesses' final wartime pantomime, in 1944, *Old Mother Red Riding Boots*, was devised by the princesses themselves with the help of the headmaster of the Royal Windsor School, Hubert Tannar.

That year, Princess Elizabeth had turned 18 and was finally old enough to join the Women's Services (though she was already an honorary colonel of the Grenadier Guards, in which capacity she undertook her first inspection of a military regiment on her 16th birthday). She chose to join the Auxiliary Territorial Service (the ATS) and trained as a driver and mechanic, with the rank of second subaltern. Photographs of the princess, dubbed 'Princess Auto Mechanic' by the press, working on engines made a valuable statement about young women's contribution to the war. After five months, she was promoted to Junior Commander. Meanwhile, Princess Margaret, who had been a Girl Guide, joined the Sea Rangers.

The Royal sisters' determination to serve alongside their father's subjects, when they might just have hidden away or even escaped over the Atlantic, would endear them to the British people for many years to come.

8

IT'S THAT MAN AGAIN!

Keeping the Nation's Children Entertained

AS THE ROYAL PRINCESSES MUST have known when they were putting on their pantomimes, keeping the nation entertained and morale high was as vital a part of the war effort as digging for victory. The BBC was at the forefront of endeavours to keep Britain's children smiling through.

Children's Hour, the Home Service programme created to appeal to children between the ages of five and 15, was broadcast every day between 5pm and 6pm. It was named after a poem with the same title by the American poet Henry Wadsworth Longfellow, which described his family's evening routine as his three daughters got ready for bed.

Among the programme's early presenters were Cecil Lewis, who became known to listeners as Uncle Caractacus, and Reginald Palmer, who was called Uncle Rex. Other early presenters included composer L. Stanton Jeffries and Arthur Burrows – Uncle Arthur – who was the BBC's first director of programmes. Scotland's own edition of the show was presented by Auntie Kathleen, broadcaster Kathleen Garscadden.

The tradition of referring to the presenters as Uncles or Aunties was officially dropped in the mid-thirties, but in 1939, *Children's Hour* was presented by Derek McCullough, who would always be Uncle Mac to his listeners. Except when he was being Larry the Lamb...

Children's Hour encompassed a number of different serials that rotated throughout the year. *Toytown*, a series of radio plays based on a book written by SG Hulme, was probably the most famous. Whenever *Children's Hour* had a Request Week, *Toytown* almost always garnered the most listener votes. The hero of *Toytown* was Larry the Lamb (voiced by Uncle Mac), who had a sausage dog sidekick called Dennis The Dachshund. The clever animals would cause havoc, taunting *Toytown*'s self-important Mr Mayor and the eternally disgruntled Mr Growser, and outwitting Ernest the Policeman.

Nature-loving listeners enjoyed *Out with Romany*, a *Children's Hour* series created by Methodist Minister the Rev George Bramwell Evens, who wrote under the pseudonym Romany or The Tramp. *Out with Romany* introduced listeners to matters of the countryside and natural history.

The Rev Evens was of Romany descent. His mother was born in a wagon, known as a vardo. Evens chronicled his travels in his own vardo, pulled by Comma the horse, and these formed the basis for his radio programme. Though the shows were scripted, they gave listeners the impression that they were a live recording of events on a walk through the countryside with Romany, his English Cocker Spaniel Raq and their friends.

Other popular series included *Norman and Henry Bones: the Boy Detectives*, an original mystery drama featuring comedian Charles Hawtrey, who would go on to star in the *Carry On* films, as Norman Bones. *Worzel Gummidge*, based on the novels by Barbara Euphan Todd, in which the eponymous scarecrow comes to life and, naturally, causes havoc, was another instant hit.

Children's Hour also contained a news segment and occasional quizzes. And while it was billed to run for a whole hour, the last five minutes were actually taken up with a very grown-up weather report.

Throughout the war, the BBC Empire Service ran a programme called *It's All Yours* which featured a section called 'Let's join the children', in which compere Helen Clare, a variety star, gave children the opportunity to send poignant messages to fathers, uncles and brothers who were serving overseas. The show was broadcast from a number of locations, including London Zoo, where Miss Clare and one of her child guests were photographed for the *Radio Times*, clinging on to the back of a camel.

Petula Clark made her very first radio appearance on the show in October 1942, aged ten, singing 'Mighty Lak a Rose' for her uncle, who was serving in Iraq. Miss Clark's performance caused such a stir that she was invited to take to the stage with Vera Lynn at the Queensbury All Services Club (now the Prince Edward Theatre) in London's West End two months later. She was soon dubbed 'Britain's Shirley Temple' and became a regular on the radio, making almost 500 appearances over the next couple of years. She made her film debut in *Medal for the General* in 1944. *It's All Yours* had launched a brilliant career.

But the BBC's wartime function wasn't only to provide entertainment. Its educational role was important too. To allow for the fact that paper shortages meant the BBC's school programmes could no longer be supplemented with accompanying pamphlets, the programming was simplified with an increased emphasis on drama and narrative to keep the interest of young listeners.

One light entertainment programme with an educational twist that was particularly popular with children and adults alike was

The Brains Trust, in which a panel of experts answered listeners' questions on any topic you could imagine from 'How will the war affect farmers' to 'How does a fly land upside down on the ceiling?' Soon after it first aired on January 1st 1941, the programme was receiving more than 4,000 letters a week.

The panel, who were not told in advance what they might be asked, originally comprised philosopher CEM Joad, biologist Professor Julian Huxley and naval Commander A B Campbell, and was chaired by question master Donald McCullough. Later guests included conductor Sir Malcolm Sargent, philosopher AJ Ayer and Sir Isaiah Berlin. There were women on the panel too, including Violet Bonham Carter (grandmother of the actress Helena Bonham Carter), actress Anna Neagle and economist Barbara Mary Ward.

For those children lucky enough not to have to go to bed straight after *Children's Hour* ended, the entertainment continued with a comedy show.

Though *It's That Man Again*, which became known as *ITMA*, was created for adults, it was very popular with younger listeners. Written by Ted Kavanagh, *ITMA* starred music hall legend Tommy Handley, supported by a cast of regular characters. 'That man' in the show's title referred to Adolf Hitler himself.

ITMA marked a departure for British comedy. It was a fast-moving and satirical sketch show, poking fun at the endless, sometimes pointless-seeming regulation that proliferated in a country at war. To make sure that every show was bang up to date, scripts were often being rewritten right up until the moment they were broadcast.

Each regular character had a catchphrase, many of which quickly entered the nation's vernacular. There was the charlady Mrs Mopp, who coined the catchphrase, 'Can I do you now, sir?' and 'Ta-ta for now', which was abbreviated to TTFN. Drunken Colonel

Chinstrap, who was forever mishearing questions and interpreting them as a suggestion that he might like a drink, was often heard to say, 'Don't mind if I do'.

Colonel Chinstrap was played by actor Jack Train, who also provided the voices for the German Funf, 'the enemy agent with the feet of sauerkraut', and Claude and Cecil, the exceedingly polite odd-job men, who didn't get much done between saying, 'After you, Cecil – no, after you, Claude.'

There were frequent, slightly surreal interruptions throughout the show by a character called The Diver, played by Horace Percival. This character, whose arrival was always heralded by the gurgling sound of a man exhaling under water, was based on Frank Gadsby, a one-legged swimmer who made a living collecting donations from people who watched him perform impressive dives from the pier at New Brighton in Merseyside. The phrases Gadsby used in real life, to prompt generosity from his audience, were used by his *ITMA* caricature too. 'Don't forget the diver, sir, don't forget the diver', and, 'Every penny makes the water warmer!' was soon heard in school playgrounds up and down the country.

ITMA provided a big boost to Britain's spirits. The character of incompetent German spy Funf ridiculed the German propaganda machine, which was extremely important at a time when many British people were tuning in to the German medium wave station Reichssender Hamburg, to hear broadcasts by 'Lord Haw Haw', who gave exaggerated reports of Allied losses in the hope of discouraging Allied troops and their families back home. Lord Haw Haw was eventually revealed to be William Joyce, an American-born fascist, who had moved to England and become a member of Oswald Mosley's British Union of Fascists.

In April 1942, the cast of *ITMA* was summoned to Windsor Castle to make a very special broadcast on the occasion of the 16th birthday of Princess Elizabeth. King George VI in particular was a huge fan of the show. It was even said, by an unnamed member of the royal household, that if the war were to end between 8.30pm and 9pm on a Thursday night, nobody would dare tell the King until *ITMA* had finished.

The BBC's light entertainment programmes brought the nation together and helped people believe that one day all would be well. In the meantime, for children like Jeannette Tomlinson, the radio was a way to tune in to a dream.

Jeanette Tomlinson, 94

THE RADIO WAS VERY IMPORTANT to me as a child. We listened to a mixture of things at home. Music, comedy, murder mysteries. I liked *ITMA*. But I especially loved Victor Silvester's dance music show – the *BBC Dancing Club*. Victor Silvester was a former world ballroom dancing champion who had his own dance band. They had a big hit with their song 'You're Dancing On My Heart'. That was their theme tune.

One of the best bits about the *Dancing Club* was that, as well as music, the show contained a proper dancing lesson. Mr Silvester would dictate the steps for the people at home to follow. When the show first started out, there would be a pause after the steps were read out so that listeners could write them down. Can you believe they discovered that Lord Haw Haw was jumping in on the pauses to broadcast his German propaganda? After the BBC found that out, Mr Silvester would repeat the steps a few times rather than let there be a silence that the Germans could use to spread their lies.

When he was at home and the *Dancing Club* was on, Dad would say, 'Come on, Jeanette. We'll learn this step together,' and we'd clear everything out of the way to make a dance floor in the kitchen.

Dad loved music. I always loved music too. Dad had a gramophone with a lid. When I was very small, I'd chewed the edge of its wooden case, leaving it with teeth marks. Later, when I was about six or seven, I would creep downstairs on a Sunday morning, put a new needle in, put the record on very low and sit with my head right inside the speaker so I could listen to it without waking anyone else up. I'd get a thing about certain records. I remember being in love with *The Continental*.

Having become interested in dancing through listening to Victor Silvester, I decided I wanted to know more. Mum was quite strict at home. We weren't allowed to run down the stairs or make a noise tearing about. She agreed to dancing lessons so that I would use up some energy, I suppose, and I was very bandy when I was little so the idea was to improve my legs. It was good for that.

I started lessons at a tuppenny-ha'penny little school, then discovered Nancy Robinson's Dancing School in Streatham. We called the principal, Miss Robinson, 'Miss Nancy'. I went to her school all the way through the war. The actress June Whitfield, famous for starring in *Terry and June* and *Absolutely Fabulous*, was a pupil of Miss Nancy too.

I loved dancing from the moment I started. I wanted to be Ginger Rogers. I did ballroom and ballet. I also learned to tap dance. Soon I was dancing whenever I had spare time, including on Saturdays. Most children went to the pictures on a Saturday morning but I was always at Miss Nancy's. My sister danced for a while too but when she was 12, Mum said she had to give it up if she didn't really want to do it because Mum couldn't afford classes for both of us.

Once my sister had given up and with my mother expecting Barry, my little brother, I used to have to go all the way to Streatham for classes on my own. In the winter, I went up and down in the blackout. There were no streetlights. I can remember walking down the middle of the road coming home. There was nobody about.

At the beginning of the war we were living in Mitcham in South London. I can remember seeing the communal shelter being built on Figges Marsh Field, the green opposite our house. While we were waiting for the shelter to be finished, we were told that if you had a cupboard under the stairs, you had to clear it out and put a little bed in there. When the first raid happened, we couldn't get in our understairs cupboard because it hadn't yet been cleared out – all our shoes were thrown in there – so we went next door and got into our neighbours' cupboard instead. We were supposed to be prepared but with two children to look after, Mum didn't have the time.

The raids were frightening initially but my parents decided we weren't going to be evacuated. Mum said that if we were to go, we would all go together! It was a fatalistic attitude that was quite common at the time.

When the Blitz really got going we had to go over to the communal shelter every night. It wasn't a very good shelter. It looked like a mound of earth from the outside. Inside, it was just a dark passageway with forms – which is what we called benches – along each wall. At tea-time each day, Mum would tell my sister and me to take our bedclothes over to the shelter and put them on a bench, so that when the warning sounded we'd be ready. We had three benches that became 'ours' for the duration: one for mum, one for my sister and one for me. How Mum slept on her narrow bench I don't know. She was quite a large lady.

Everyone on the street used the shelter so there was always plenty of company but there was nothing much going on in there. You couldn't have a cup of tea or anything like that. And when it rained, the shelter got flooded so that you couldn't use the benches. They put up bunk beds eventually. We had three of those but when the shelter flooded, you couldn't use the bottom bunk either. It was so horrible in there we stopped going after a while.

One night a bomb did drop near the shelter. It blew a couple of windows out in nearby houses but there was no serious damage and no-one was hurt. It might have been a real disaster but because it fell on the marshy grassland, it didn't properly explode.

Dad was called up quite late in the war, much to his surprise because he was over 40. He was practically a grandfather in 1940s terms but as the war went on they had to call up older men. He became a Royal Marine and was sent to the Orkney Isles for training. Mum was pregnant when he left, then my grandmother died so Mum decided we'd move in with Grandfather to look after him. He had an Anderson shelter in the back garden, so at least we didn't have to sleep on flooded bunkbeds any more.

Shortly after Dad was called up, Mum gave birth to my little brother Barry. It must have been hard for Mum having a baby in wartime amidst all the shortages and with her husband being away.

In 1944, I got a scholarship with the Royal Academy of Dancing so as well as going to Streatham to Miss Nancy's, I had to go up to Shepherd's Bush twice a week. I caught the trolley bus to Shepherd's Bush Green, then had to walk all the way up Holland Park Avenue to the big Victorian house where the RAD was housed.

This was around the time of the V2s. They were horrible. There was no warning with them. Just an explosion. They were landing all over south London. If you were out and about when the Germans were sending them over, there was always the chance you might not be coming home. But though I was only 12, I wasn't scared. Going on my own to those dance classes, I got to see a bit more of the world. There were many more people in uniform, of course.

I didn't enjoy ordinary school – I went to the Links Road Senior school in Tooting, which was girls only back then. It was three storeys high and in between lessons there were prefects on every stairway to make sure you didn't make a racket going up to the top.

When I started, I thought it was a huge building but looking at it later, I realised it wasn't that big at all.

Somehow, in my last year there, I was elected head girl. Don't ask me why! I couldn't wait to leave. As soon as I could I walked out of the school gates for good and started working as a student teacher at my dancing school.

VE day went by in a blur but a year later, I took part in a show for the 1946 Victory celebrations at the Kings Theatre in Hammersmith.

That same year, I went on my first theatre tour. My teacher thought I ought to do panto as experience for my own teaching. I got a part in *Aladdin* with Clarkson Rose, an English comedian who specialised in playing the pantomime dame. He'd worked with ENSA – the Entertainments National Service Association – during the war, going all over the place to entertain the troops. ENSA sometimes had a nickname – Every Night Something Awful – but Clarkson Rose was very popular.

The first time I went to rehearse, my mother came with me and waited in the dressing room to make sure everything went well, but after that I was on my own. Thelma, my friend from dance school, was in the panto too, which helped my parents feel happy that I'd be safe on the tour. It was my first experience of a big audience.

After the panto, we had a couple of weeks off, then Clarkson Rose asked if I'd like to go on another tour. This time it was with his famous Twinkle Revue company, which had played all through the war, starring people like Tommy Fields, who was brother to the more famous Gracie.

Twinkle was a different kind of show. I was one of a group of dancers called 'The Clarkson Rosebuds'. There were four of us to begin with. Mr Rose and his wife Olive Fox, who was a star in her own right, ensured every costume was pristine and the very best.

Our hair and every aspect of our appearance had to look the very best.

Twinkle featured a lot of headliners of the revue days. We were on the same bill as so many of the 'variety' greats. The revues contained music popular at the time from Noel Coward to Ivor Novello. The dance routines were carefully choreographed and we were forever learning new steps. Tap, ballet, ballroom, the lot. Some of the dances were awful. I remember the 'Pony Trot' and when we were 'Puppets on a String'. I hated those. However most dances were lovely to do and if it was your birthday, the musical director would add 'Happy Birthday' into the theme. The show had speciality dancers too, including Wilson, Keppel and Betty who were famous for their 'Sand Dance'. Pre-war they'd performed in Berlin and been condemned as indecent by Goebbels himself!

One of the comics in Twinkle was Norman Vaughan, who'd served in the Far East and appeared in military reviews with Spike Milligan and Harry Secombe. Harry Secombe was in our show. Then there was Billy Burden, who was from the West Country and specialised in playing the 'local yokel'. He had a beautiful singing voice. When we started the Twinkle tour he didn't actually have a singing part in it but they got him to do a song and after that he would get encore after encore. The audience wouldn't let him go back to his dressing room. In the 1980s, he appeared in *Hi-De-Hi!* Sometimes there would be guests. Terry Scott (of *Terry and June*), joined us in Hastings.

The boarding houses and digs where we stayed were full of characters and I could write a book about some of those experiences. I recall having to get special ration cards from the food office as I was on tour. In Stratford upon Avon, there were a lot of us in digs. We used to give the landlady our ration cards and she'd give each of us our weekly four ounces of butter in a little dish. You had to remember which was yours and use it carefully through the week.

Being one of Clarkson's Rose Buds changed my life, I met my husband Wally Tomlinson, a scouser with a good sense of humour, through Twinkle. He sang and was a wonderful 'siffleur' – that is to say, a professional whistler. An announcement for our 1952 wedding said, 'Stars for a Day, Jeanette Leech and Wally Tomlinson will Twinkle Down the Aisle at St Olave's Church. Supported by Clarkson Rose, Olive Fox and all the company.' I miss him very much but have very happy memories.

I danced all the way through the war and I still do a little dancing now. In my sixties, I appeared on stage and TV with my dance troupe The Jelly Rolls. In 1995, for the 50th anniversary of VE Day, we performed at the British Legion's gala concert in Hyde Park alongside Dame Vera Lynn and Sir Cliff Richard. Well into my eighties, I was going to Zumba classes run by my daughter.

I often look back on the war and the years immediately afterwards and hope that, amidst all the rationing and greyness, I helped to bring some colour and entertainment.

9

BIGGLES, WORRALS
AND MUMFIE

Wartime Books, Toys And Games

AFTER THE FIRE SERVICE, THE police and the Red Cross had been and gone, bombsites became popular playgrounds for the war babies. For the girls, the derelict houses were the perfect place to play at 'Mummies and Daddies' with a real kitchen sink, while the boys roamed the wreckage, engaged in mock battles, shooting at each other through blown out windows and doors. Bombsites were also a great place to hunt for prized pieces of shrapnel to be shown off at school.

It goes without saying that such playgrounds were not without danger. Throughout the war and well into the decades that followed, children were injured and even killed while playing on uncleared bombsites. But perhaps it's no surprise that children wanted to play games that echoed the war going on around them – to help them make sense of it all – and toy manufacturers and publishers capital-ised on this desire with war-themed books and toys.

There was no shortage of exciting wartime reading material for all ages. For the early reader, Raphael Tuck and sons published a picture book, *Boo-Boo The Barrage Balloon*, in which a plucky male barrage balloon defended the British skies. Boo-Boo had a female equivalent called Blossom, born to 'two happily married balloons', who had her own book – *Blossom the Brave Balloon*, by E F Herbert and Philip Zee. In both stories, the barrage balloons were awarded medals for their courage, which were pinned to their silvery chests in a somewhat dangerous fashion.

For older readers, Richmal Crompton's hero William, of the *Just William* stories, exemplified the wartime spirit in children's fiction. In 1938, the author had chronicled the rise of fascism in *William The Dictator*. In 1939, she published *William and Air Raid Precautions*. This was followed by *William Does His Bit* and *William Carries On*.

The evacuee experience was chronicled in *Visitors From London* by Kitty Barne. Ms Barne had first-hand knowledge of Operation Pied Piper having helped to man a Sussex reception centre in her capacity as a member of the Women's Voluntary Service. Her book followed the adventures of the Farrar children, who are spending their holidays in the country with their aunt Myra when 17 Cockney evacuees are billeted in the farmhouse next door.

Possibly the most famous wartime books were the *Biggles* series, featuring pilot James Charles Bigglesworth, by Captain WE Johns, who had himself flown in World War One. Biggles had a female equivalent in Worrals, Flight Officer Joan Worralson, of the Women's Auxiliary Air Force, whom Captain Johns modelled on his friends, pioneering women pilots Amy Johnson and Pauline Gower. *Worrals of the WAAF* was created in response to a request from the Air Ministry for a novel that might encourage young women to consider a career in the air force.

Considering he was the nation's bogeyman, Hitler featured fairly infrequently in Britain's wartime children's books. The Fuhrer did make one memorable appearance in Kathleen Tozer's 1942 book

Mumfie Marches On, in which a toy elephant – the eponymous Mumfie – joins the Home Guard. With the help of his friends, Jelly, Ivan and Scarecrow, Mumfie captures sweet-toothed Hitler by enticing him into a giant rat trap baited with a delicious cream bun.

Meanwhile, Scottish publishing company, DC Thomson, was doing great business with its comics, which reflected the nation's wartime preoccupations by mocking the enemy (and their accents). The *Dandy* ran a cartoon strip entitled *Addie and Hermy, the Nasty Nazis,* while the *Beano* featured *Musso the Wop – He's a Big-a-da-Flop.*

In her weekly comic, *Sunny Stories,* Enid Blyton, who was yet to write her *Famous Five* series, was careful not to ape the casual xenophobia of the *Beano* and the *Dandy*. In 1940, she published a story called *The Boy Who Changed His Name,* about an unfortunate child called Adolph, who is picked on by other children who later learn the error of their ways.

Ironically, the work of one of Germany's best loved children's authors, was more readily available in wartime to British children than to their German counterparts. Dresden-born Erich Kästner's novel *Emil and the Detectives*, was very popular in the UK. In Germany, it was the only one of pacifist Kästner's books that had not been banned or burned under Nazi censorship rules.

With metal, rubber, plastics and wood all needed for the war effort, new wartime toys were hard to come by and those that were available were often made with paper and card. Most children improvised with the materials they had to hand, playing games like five stones and pick-up sticks. Grids for battleships and hopscotch were drawn out in chalk on the pavement.

Skipping games were always popular and were often accompanied by macabre rhymes and chants. Some were specially adapted for war time, such as: Sister Susie's sewing socks for soldiers.

Another rhyme, called 'Charlie Chaplin', contained the lines, 'Salute to the Captain, Bow to the Queen, And turn your back on the Nazi submarine!'

Even with the war colouring every aspect of everyday life, Harrogate war baby Ann Hay recalled, 'For children it was a much more innocent age. We could go out and play with no fear of "stranger danger". There must have been perverts but no-one warned us of them and we were fearless... our parents weren't worried so long as we were back for tea. It was rare for children to have watches – we seemed to know either "stomach-clock" or the position of the sun.'

This degree of freedom was also familiar to young Londoner Tony Lee, growing up in wartime Wandsworth.

Tony Lee, 88

EVEN WHILE THE BLITZ WAS happening, life went on in London. We were just normal kids, despite what was going on every night.

We played out in the street whenever we could: football and hopscotch and 'Knock Down Ginger'. We'd hammer on our neighbours' doors then run off before they could come out and catch us. The front doors to the houses on our street were arranged in pairs and sometimes we'd put string round the handles of two doors that were side by side, tying them together so that the people who lived there couldn't get out to chase after us when we knocked. We must have driven everyone mad.

Another game we played was 'Follow My Leader'. My friend Jimmy Johnson, who lived a couple of doors down from us, was always the leader somehow. He'd make us do all sorts of silly things. Once we were making mischief and an adult came out to tell us off. We all ran away but Jimmy got caught. He put his hands in the air and said, 'I surrender.' Then he shouted, 'Come on Tony, come on Mike,' giving the rest of us away too. It was like that scene from Dad's Army, when Captain Mainwaring accidentally reveals Private Pike's name to the German U-boat captain. 'Don't tell him, Pike!'

In the autumn, it was time for conkers. A man would come down our street with a wheelbarrow full of conkers he'd collected from Battersea Park and we'd choose the best ones to use in our battles. You weren't supposed to do anything to them before you attached them to a string but I would secretly bake mine to make them harder and more difficult to break.

My dad was in the Navy. He served on *HMS Caprice*, a C-Class destroyer. She was part of the 6th Destroyer Flotilla and took part in the Russian and the Atlantic convoys. At the end of the war, she went to the Far East.

One night during the Blitz, when Dad was home on leave, the air raid siren sounded and we all went to the communal shelter down the road. Mum, my brother and me went straight on in but Dad stood in the entrance, refusing to come inside while the Germans and the RAF were battling it out overhead. The ARP warden in charge of our neighbourhood told him, 'Come into the shelter, Mr Lee,' but Dad refused and stayed standing in the entrance like the big 'I am', with his arms folded across his chest, just watching the show up above.

Then all of a sudden, a bomb dropped in the street and the blast lifted Dad right off his feet and blew him backwards through the shelter door. He landed on his backside and we all burst out laughing. Then the ARP warden said to him, all dead-pan, 'I told you to come inside, Mr Lee.'

Our street – Quinton Street – wasn't very long but it was a street divided even in the war. At one end you had the rich families and at the other end you had the rest of us. For the VE Day party, everyone came together to celebrate and it didn't matter how rich or poor anybody was. We all mucked in together. But as soon as that one day was over, everything went back to normal and the rich kids didn't talk to the poor kids anymore. It was a good place to live though. We didn't feel like we missed out on anything because nobody had very much. When I look back at the friendships I had and the mischief we made, I think they were happy times.

10

MOONLIGHT SONATA

The Coventry Blitz

BETWEEN SEPTEMBER 1940 AND MAY 1941, the Luftwaffe targeted all of the United Kingdom's most strategically important cities.

Coventry, in the West Midlands, was always going to be on the hit list. It was a major manufacturing hub, home to dozens of factories. During the First World War the city had ramped up its capacity to supply armaments. When that conflict ended, Coventry was at the forefront of Britain's burgeoning motor industry, but in the last years of the 1930s most of the city's factories were turned over to war production again.

By 1940, the Coventry factories of Hawker Siddeley, Vickers-Armstrongs, Rolls Royce and Armstrong Whitworth were all producing engines and other parts for aeroplanes. Daimler and Humber pivoted from making luxury cars to armoured vehicles. Dunlop, which had supplied tyres, made barrage balloons to baffle the enemy fighter planes. Courtaulds, the textile company, began to produce parachute silk. GEC concentrated on military radio equipment. Meanwhile, the Coventry Ordnance Works was one of the largest centres for munitions in the country.

With such a concentration of industry, there was no doubt that a successful raid on Coventry could severely hamper the British war effort. From the very beginning of the war, the Government expected that Coventry, like London and Manchester and Britain's port cities, would be a target for the German bombers.

As it happened, Coventry had had some practice in dealing with bombings before. In August 1939, just nine days before the outbreak of war, the IRA had detonated explosives in Broadgate, one of the city's main shopping streets, killing five and injuring many more. So perhaps the city was braced for more such violence. With their gas masks slung around their necks or over their shoulders, the people of Coventry 'kept calm and carried on'.

The Germans did not attack Coventry straight away and throughout the 'Phoney War' the people of Coventry were left largely untroubled. It wasn't until August 1940 that Coventry saw its first air raid. There were 17 small raids on the city over the two months after that, killing 176. But Coventry's true night of terror, when it finally came, unfolded in a way that no-one had really expected.

The Luftwaffe had excellent maps of the city and would therefore have known that the factories most valuable to the war effort were all located on Coventry's outskirts. There was nothing of strategic value in the streets around the historic medieval cathedral. No reason to target them.

However, on November 8th, the RAF carried out a daring bombing raid on Munich, which changed everything about Hitler's approach to dealing with the British. While the raid on Munich had not caused huge damage to the German war machine, the psychological effect was much more significant. Munich was the spiritual home of the Nazi Party and Hitler took the news that the city had been bombed especially badly.

In the days that followed, the Führer planned revenge. The bombing of Coventry, with a raid code-named *Unternehmen*

Mondscheinsonate' (Operation Moonlight Sonata), was designed to inflict maximum pain on the city's civilians. Coventry's factories may still have been the official target (indeed that's how Hitler would justify his actions) but the Fuhrer knew that a raid on Coventry's city centre – her shops, her beautiful medieval buildings, and her beloved cathedral – would hit Coventry's people, and the rest of the people of Britain, right in the heart.

On November 14th, less than a week after the RAF's daring raid on Munich, Hitler was ready to retaliate.

Operation Moonlight Sonata was chillingly methodical. The first planes to fly over dropped pathfinder flares, to illuminate the Luftwaffe's targets. Not that they needed those flares. Though Coventry was under blackout as usual, the full moon shone brightly overhead, like an enormous floodlight, exactly as Hitler and his High Command had hoped. After the pathfinders came 500 bombers, flying first from north to south, before they changed direction and crossed the city again from east to west, to ensure that not an inch of the historic centre was left unscathed.

That night's raid lasted for 11 hours, during which the Luftwaffe dropped 500 tons of high explosive, some 30,000 incendiaries and dozens of parachute mines. They also deployed a new weapon, an exploding incendiary, for the very first time. Several were dropped on the Daimler works, causing a fire that raged over 15 acres and was all but impossible to put out. To the desperate rescue workers, who were called in from all over the Midlands, it must have seemed as though the whole of Coventry was ablaze.

Operation Moonlight Sonata was the most highly concentrated German attack on any British city during the war. More than half the city's homes were damaged or lost that night, displacing tens of thousands of people. The newly homeless wandered the streets in confusion, asking themselves, 'What now?'

As Coventry pulled itself from the rubble, the official death toll rose to 554, though it's possible that many of the raid's victims were never accounted for. More than 400 suffered life-changing injuries.

In the very middle of the city, the devastation was heart-breaking. A statue of the city's famous mascot, Peeping Tom – the young man who once watched Lady Godiva ride naked through Coventry's streets – had been blown from its niche. In the confusion and the dusty gloom, rescue workers thought Tom's statue was another corpse. Meanwhile Owen Owen on Broadgate, Coventry's biggest and best department store, had been hit by an incendiary bomb, which caused so much damage that the store would have to be bulldozed. And when George V saw the damage to the city's ancient and beautiful cathedral, Britain's monarch could not hold back his tears.

In what would have been a moment of terrible irony, the Cathedral came close to losing its tower, the only part of the medieval building that was still standing, not to Luftwaffe but to the demolition crew sent to make the building safe. The engineers, who were unfamiliar with the city, were unaware that the tower had been leaning since time immemorial. The cathedral tower's slanting aspect might have had nothing to do with the German bombers but the Coventry Blitz was so utterly devastating that the Luftwaffe invented a new verb, *coventrieren*, to describe the act of razing a city to the ground.

In the years that followed, the Coventry Blitz became a sore subject for the government as conspiracy theories began to circulate. Postwar, it was repeatedly claimed that Churchill had been given several days' notice of the raid but did not act on that information because doing so would have given away the fact that Bletchley Park had finally found a way to break the Germans' Enigma Code. To protect that enormous breakthrough, Coventry had to be sacrificed.

The truth is more complicated. Bletchley Park did indeed decrypt messages regarding *Operation Moonlight Sonata* as early as November 12th, but while they knew that an attack was imminent, they did not know its target. It was expected that it would be London or the Home Counties. Not Coventry. Intelligence gained from the interrogation of a downed German pilot, who did actually say that the target would be Birmingham or Coventry, was discounted as unreliable.

On the morning of November 14th 1940, Churchill was briefed about the expected attack but even at this late stage the intelligence suggested that London was in the cross-hairs. It seemed so likely that London was the target that Churchill insisted on staying in the city, to stand with the people of the capital. Churchill was reassured that, in the event that the intelligence was wrong, measures had already been taken to ensure that Birmingham, Coventry and Britain's other major cities, would be sent reinforcements from the fire and civil defence services of their neighbours. Every possible precaution was in place.

As dusk fell, Churchill and his government waited for the attack on London to begin, but that night the capital city was quiet.

As soon as it became clear that in fact Coventry was *Moonlight Sonata's* target, the Air Ministry swung into action, bombing the air bases in Cherbourg whence they believed the German bombers were coming. Meanwhile, RAF fighter planes flew to engage the Germans over the city. Coventry was already ringed by anti-aircraft guns – more than five times as many per head of population as there were in London – but it was still not enough to hold the Luftwaffe back. The incendiary bombs, never seen before, were more than the best British planning could deal with. Whatever the true story behind the raid, the devastation was immense and it would echo down the years, particularly in the lives of Coventry's children, like young Cynthia Smith.

Cynthia Smith, 87

I'VE LIVED IN COVENTRY MY whole life. From the top of my street in Canley, you can see all of the city's 'three spires'. When the war began, we were living right in the centre of the city, near the canal.

My parents weren't Coventry people. My dad Harry's family came from 'the Potteries', Stoke on Trent. My maternal side came from Austria. According to family legend, my maternal grandfather was a gardener, who came over to England with the Kaiser. His daughter, my mum, Minnie 'Min' Lenz, was born in England and grew up in London. She sounded like a proper cockney.

When Mum and Dad met, Dad was in the army. After a whirlwind romance, Mum travelled up to Stoke to meet his family. She wanted to make a good impression on her future in-laws so she wore her best dress and a pair of white gloves. But white gloves weren't a good choice for the Potteries. When she got off the train, she took one look at the factory towers belching black smoke and decided to take the next train straight back home. Dad had to be quick to catch her before she crossed to the southbound platform. It took all his charm to persuade her to stay but they were married not long after.

Dad left the army in 1936. His years in the service hadn't been exemplary. He was 'had up' before the military court a couple of times for being drunk and disorderly, so it was probably for the best he went back to civilian life. Unfortunately, he left the army at exactly the wrong time because there wasn't much work to be had. To make matters worse, Mum was pregnant with their first child – my big sister Chris. Because there was no money to pay for Mum's maternity care, she had to give birth in the hospital wing of the Stoke on Trent Union Work House.

With another mouth to feed, Dad needed a job more urgently than ever, so he looked into moving away from Stoke to the Midlands. Coventry was doing well so Dad moved Mum and Chris down there and started working as a postman.

The house they moved to was a little terraced house on Leicester Causeway, a street running along the Coventry Canal, in Foleshill near the city centre. Mum and Dad rented number 14. It was last but one in the terrace. On the other side of the last house, was a single-story ramshackle building which everyone called 'the cottage'. Directly across the road was Turrall's Garage. There were lots of car factories around Coventry back then, with all the big British names having bases in the city.

When Mum became pregnant again – with me – she was determined that this time she would not be giving birth in a work house. I was born at home on the evening of November 14th 1938.

I was too young to notice much of what went on in the run-up to the war but I know a large bomb shelter was set up at the back of Turrall's Garage for all the residents of Leicester Causeway to use. Dad wasn't convinced. Plenty of people didn't believe that the shelters, which had been put up so quickly, really were safe. And if the shelters themselves were safe, what about the people you'd find in them? Many husbands didn't like the idea that while they were off in the forces, their wives and children might be spending the night in the dark with strange men. When it came to protecting us from the Luftwaffe, Dad decided we would be safer at home.

Dad had been recalled to the army and was being sent to Scotland, but before he went, he reinforced the cupboard under the stairs at number 14, fitting it out with carpet and a light. He put a mattress in there, where Mum, Chris and I could sleep. If the air raid siren sounded, that was where we had to go. Apart from anything else, Dad told us that if the worst happened, he didn't want to spend days searching for us. He wanted to know exactly where we were.

When the raids started, we spent night after night under the stairs. Mum would put us to bed, then stay in the kitchen, doing her mending, until the sirens sounded or one of us cried. Then Mum would crawl into the cubby hole to spend the rest of the night beside us. Each morning, the neighbours would ask why we hadn't joined them in the shelter behind Turrall's. Mum always told them that we were perfectly safe under the stairs. Until we weren't.

November 14th 1940 was my second birthday. With Dad away in Scotland, training new army recruits on anti-aircraft guns, Mum did her best to make the day special. There was a cake, made within the rations – with candles, of course – and at least a dozen birthday cards from friends and neighbours. Mum lined the cards up on the mantelpiece. After a nice birthday tea, Mum put me and Chris, who was now four, to bed under the stairs.

Nightfall came early in November and as soon as it did, the German bombers would follow. When the air-raid sounded, our neighbours hurried to the shelter behind Turrall's Garage but, as usual, we stayed put. Most people had given up worrying about us. If Mum and Dad didn't want us to be in the shelter, that was their business. However that night, Mr Turrall, the owner of the garage, wasn't happy about it.

Mr Turrall decided he'd had enough. He wasn't going to let Mum and me and Chris stay under the stairs another night. He marched across the street and hammered on the door until Mum answered. He told her, 'I'm not having it, Min. You're coming to the shelter with the rest of us. I don't care what Harry says. It's not about him. It's about you and the girls.' And for the first time ever Mum gave in. She scooped us up and followed Mr Turrall across the road. I think she was secretly glad he wouldn't take 'no' for an answer.

In the shelter behind Turrall's garage, we huddled together, wrapped in our blankets. My birthday was forgotten as everyone listened out for the sound of German bombers overhead.

The raid went on all night. No-one in the shelter got any sleep. Me and Chris were both crying. We'd never been so frightened in our lives. Mum tried to keep us calm but everybody was in a right state. All the adults knew this was something different to the other raids.

When the all-clear sounded in the early morning, everyone went out onto the street to see how bad things were. Was it as bad as it had sounded? Although it was November, it was really warm from all the fires that were still burning. And though the sun was up, it was dark too, because of all the smoke and dust.

As soon as we stepped outside, Mum must have realised how lucky we'd been. Our house was still standing but only just. The house next door had taken a direct hit. The lean-to cottage was gone. There was nothing left but a pile of smoking rubble. It must have been a real shock to Mum to see how close the bombers got. It was a wake-up call, alright.

It was too risky to stay in the house while next door was still smouldering and no-one knew what structural damage had been done. Someone looked after me and Chris while Min went inside to fetch a few necessities.

Most of the windows were broken and everything was covered in dust. Mum told us later that the pictures had fallen off the walls. And all my birthday cards had been blown off the mantelpiece. Adolf Hitler ruined my birthday. He's ruined every birthday I've had since because every November 14th I have to think of him.

While our neighbours tried to get back to normal, we couldn't live in our house so we joined some other evacuees on a farm outside the city, where we hoped we would be safer. Chris loved the country life. When we were adults, she moved to live on a farm for good.

When we were able to go back home, we got used to living in the middle of a bombsite. We had to walk through devastated streets every day. It would take a long time for Coventry to be put back together.

At the end of the war, we had a VE Day street party to celebrate. A long table was laid down the middle of the road, covered with all the food and drink people could spare for the occasion. A reporter from the *Coventry Evening Telegraph* came to take a photograph for the newspaper. Me and Chris were sitting near the end of the table closest to the photographer, with our hair in matching ringlets tied up with ribbons.

Everyone used up their rations to make the party food. I'd never seen so much food in my life. Mum made some jellies for us to take along to share, though when Dad heard what she'd done he was really angry, because no-one was supposed to know we had them. He'd pinched those jellies from the army stores.

In the newspaper photograph, Mum is behind us with the rest of the mothers, all looking older than their years, no doubt through the strain of the war. They've got their backs to the pile of rubble that was once our neighbours' house and 'the cottage'. Four and a half years had passed since the Blitz, but neither had been rebuilt.

They never were. We used to play on that bomb site. Years later, my two sons played on it too, when we all came to live with Mum and Dad after my divorce.

I don't know what happened to the family who lived in the house next door in 1940. I suppose they were given one of the pre-fabs that sprung up all over the place immediately after the war. When I married my second husband, we lived in a pre-fab. It was made of tin. Freezing cold in the winter and boiling hot in the summer. They were only supposed to be up for a few years, but a few are still standing today.

A couple of months after that VE Day party with the stolen jelly, Dad was demobbed from the army. I remember the day he came home. I was used to it being just the three of us: me, Mum and Chris. When Dad was around, it changed everything. Mum didn't have as much time for me and my sister. All her attention was on Dad and I hated that. So on the day that he came home from the war, when I saw him turning into our street, I ran inside and shouted, 'Mum, that horrible man is coming!' I thought we should hide under the stairs.

I did get over it, of course, and came to love Dad as much as I loved Mum. Dad nicknamed me 'Blitzy' because of my birthday but we were a lucky family. We all survived. We didn't lose anybody. Dad came home and we just got on with things. Everybody from Coventry knows someone who had it worse in the war. We had a happy life.

I didn't used to think the war had touched me all that much. Like I said, there were others who had it much worse – who lost their families and their homes. The only way I thought it affected me was that I never looked forward to my birthday, knowing it was also the anniversary of so much suffering, and I never liked having candles on my cake because of the smell. That whiff from a candle that's just been blown out takes me straight back to 1940 and being in the shelter during the Coventry Blitz.

It's the smell I can never forget. I only have to look at a photograph of a bomb site and it's in my nose again. I can't get rid of it. It's the smell of gas and smoke and burning and brick dust. But I wouldn't have said I had any trauma about the Blitz or anything like that. Not until something strange happened, years and years later.

It was nearly 75 years later, in fact. I was on a Mediterranean cruise with my partner Tony, to celebrate his 80th birthday.

We'd been having a lovely time. On our way back home, the ship docked in Gibraltar and we went onshore to see the monkeys on the Rock. Me and Tony were sitting on a wall, having our photograph taken with some of the monkeys behind us when, out of nowhere, a plane suddenly flew right over our heads. It was a military plane and it was flying really fast and low. The noise of the engines was deafening. And that was when I lost it. I just completely lost it. It took me totally by surprise. I started shaking and crying and I just couldn't stop. Long after the plane was gone, I was still sobbing. We had to abandon the day trip and Tony took me back to the ship.

I knew in my head that I was safe. That plane wasn't coming to attack us. No-one was going to bomb me now. But inside I was all over the place. I was back in Coventry again, two years old and in the shelter, hearing the Germans flying over, dropping bombs left, right and centre. How my mother coped, bringing me and Christine up, with all that going on, I don't know. Mothers in war have to be as brave as any soldier.

It had never happened to me before, that sort of reaction to the sound of a plane, and it hasn't happened since. I don't know why it came back to me that day in particular but as I get older, I feel closer to those parts of my past than I used to and I'm more careful now about things that might remind me. Like the smell of candles on a birthday cake.

11

LONDON'S BURNING

The Second Great Fire of London

AS THE PEOPLE OF COVENTRY mourned the loss of their beautiful cathedral, another iconic cathedral was in danger. On the night of December 29th-30th 1940, more than 100,000 bombs fell on the City of London, the capital's financial and business centre.

The targets for this particular attack were uniquely vulnerable. This time, the Germans were focussing on a part of London with many commercial and public buildings that were not large enough to have the compulsory round-the-clock fire-watchers demanded by recent government legislation. The result was that, by using small incendiaries, the Germans were able to start around 1,500 individual fires in unprotected buildings, quickly stretching the fire brigade and the ARP to the very limit.

To add to the difficulty of the firefighters' mission, a strong wind fanned the City that night, whipping the flames ever higher. At the same time, a water pipe coming into the City was fractured by a bomb, causing a shortage of mains water, while a low tide hampered efforts to pump water from the River Thames. The attack must have been timed to take advantage of that fact.

Many of London's most valuable historic buildings were caught up in the firestorm. The medieval Guildhall was badly damaged.

Paternoster Row, which was at that time the centre of London's publishing trade, was razed to the ground. Twenty publishing houses were destroyed or badly damaged, with the loss of more than five million books in a painful echo of the Nazi Party's mania for book-burning back home in Germany.

The City had not been in such danger of total annihilation since the Great Fire of 1666. This really was the Second Great Fire of London. American war correspondent Ernie Pyle described it as, 'the most hateful, most beautiful single scene I have ever known.' The city, he wrote, was 'ringed and stabbed with fire'.

As the firefighters battled the flames, alongside the ARP, the police, soldiers and brave civilian volunteers, it seemed inevitable that the ring of fire would engulf Sir Christopher Wren's masterpiece, St Paul's Cathedral. The cathedral was the very emblem of the City, having risen from the ashes of the earlier Gothic cathedral of the same name, which was burned in 1666.

St Paul's had its own fire service of sorts - the St Paul's Watch, a group of more than 300 assorted staff, clergy, architects and local residents, all under the captaincy of Godfrey Allen, who was the cathedral's surveyor to the Fabric. They were ready on the cathedral's roof, armed with buckets of sand. In the Crypt was a first aid post, staffed by more volunteers, mainly women. The Watchers had already saved the cathedral from a direct hit from a high explosive bomb in October. Would they be able to save her again as the flames drew closer?

The demonic glow that lit up the sky could be seen for miles around. Even as far away as Grays in Essex where Rosemary Ball watched from the safety of her mother's arms.

Rosemary Ball, 85

WHEN I WAS GROWING UP, my mum would often tell me about the night the City of London was set alight and we nearly lost St Paul's. She said we could see the horizon glowing red from the garden of our uncle's house in Grays, which was where we were staying at the time. She might even have described it as beautiful, if she hadn't known what was making the sky look so strange.

My family lived in Albert Square in Lambeth. Not the one in *EastEnders* but something very similar-looking. My dad had been a Royal Marine in the First World War. Mum was a lady's maid. I was their first child, born at the beginning of the war. When the Blitz started, Dad decided to take me and Mum to the country where we lived with his brother's family. My uncle was too old to be in the armed forces but his wife was in the Land Army and their son was away fighting.

I was very young when we got there but I do have a few very vivid memories. The bungalow where we lived was right across the road from the air raid siren so we always got the full force of the noise. We called that siren 'Moaning Minnie'. For some reason the sound Moaning Minnie made for the 'All Clear' – long and drawn out – was worse than the noise it made to tell you the Germans were on their way. From down the lane came more noise from an 'ack-ack' gun, while a searchlight strobed the clouds. We did see planes flying overhead, following the line of the river Thames, to avoid the barrage balloons. And once, I remember Mum and I standing in the garden together, looking back towards London, where smoke was hanging in the sky. That must have been around the time of the doodlebugs or the V2s.

When the raids weren't happening, we had a quiet life. Dad's brother was a baker, so he always had flour. We never had to worry about bread. We grew vegetables and at the end of the road was a pig sty. A group of people had got together to raise the pig and we would all take our food scraps down to feed it. I enjoyed doing that. I don't remember ever feeling hungry though I do recall my Dad telling me that my pet rabbit had to be 'put to sleep'. I've got a feeling we had him for lunch!

Eighty years on, it's funny what stays with you. I can still remember the sound of 'Moaning Minnie'. I don't know where that name came from. I've never met anyone else whose family called the siren that, but that's what she'll always be to me.

12

BUSINESS AS USUAL

A New Wave of Evacuations

THE SECOND GREAT FIRE OF London encompassed an even larger area than the first. The devastation was heartbreaking. Thirty-one guild halls and 19 churches, including 13 built by Wren were destroyed. The human cost was unbearable. Across the City, 160 civilians were killed, including 14 firefighters.

Astonishingly, though it was struck by at least 28 incendiary bombs, St Paul's Cathedral survived. Newspapers reported on the bravery the city's residents continued to show under fire. 'London Can Take It!' proclaimed a propaganda film of the time and the government pushed the idea of the Blitz Spirit to lift the nation's morale. But as 1940 drew to a close, Britain was reeling from four months of non-stop aerial bombardment. Though shops in Britain's bombed out cities defiantly displayed signs proclaiming 'business as usual', the country's infrastructure was creaking.

Utility supplies were frequently disrupted by the air raids. Schools that hadn't already been relocated in their entirety were barely able to operate. There was a serious housing crisis. Many London parents in particular began to reconsider their decision not to evacuate their children (or to have brought them back too soon) and another wave of evacuations took place. By February

1941, the number of official evacuees reached its peak at 1.37 million. Among the children sent to the country after the Blitz became too much to bear were Sylvia Lee and her two big brothers.

Sylvia Lee, 86

I'VE LIVED ON THE SAME street in Earlsfield ever since I was born. The brick shelter in the back garden has been there for about the same length of time as me – 86 years. I came into the world in 1939. My mum and dad were Elsie and Leslie and I had two big brothers – Leslie and Stan.

Though we did have that shelter in our garden, I mostly remember going into the public shelter on Garratt Lane, where there were bunkbeds arranged in rows for us to sleep in. We must have been in there instead of our shelter because our street was badly bombed. Three houses on our side and a couple on the other were demolished. The local primary school got bombed too. The damage was so bad that the top floor had to be taken down.

On one occasion, late in the Blitz, my brother Stan and I were sitting on the stairs leading up to the flat – the one I still live in now– when a bomb fell nearby. The explosion shattered the skylight above us and Stan and I were both covered in glass. I'm not sure how we managed to get out of that unscathed. We should have been cut to pieces. I don't think we cried. We were in too much shock.

Perhaps it was the skylight blowing in that made Mum have a change of heart and think we would be better off being evacuated. I was sent to Norfolk, which is where her side of the family came from. I think I went to stay with my gran but she was too old to look after a toddler, so I ended up being cared for by two ladies who lived in a big old house. I didn't like it. The kitchen had a bare wooden floor and there was a big fireplace with big beetles crawling all over it. I suppose they must have come in with the logs. The ladies I lived with weren't half so bothered by the beetles as I was, but they definitely objected when I brought frogs in from the garden!

I have one very clear memory of being in Norfolk, clinging to the school railings. I was crying because the local school children kept shouting 'Say something, Sylvia!' Sounds innocent enough but I just stood there and shook my head because I knew they only wanted me to talk so they could laugh at my London accent. To think they thought I was the one who sounded funny!

I was very, very unhappy as an evacuee and Mum really fretted with me being so small and so far away, so though the bombs were still falling, she came and fetched me home. She soon went to fetch my brother Stan too.

Leslie, having been born in 1926, was old enough to sign up before the war ended. He joined the navy and went to sea on *HMS Vengeance*, an aircraft carrier. He didn't see any fighting but towards the end of the war, *Vengeance* went to the Far East. I've got a picture of Leslie in Kowloon in Hong Kong. Though he was never in a battle, I know one thing that really affected him was seeing the prisoners of war, newly liberated from the Japanese camps, who were in a terrible state through malnutrition and disease. Some of them had been horribly tortured. Leslie himself contracted malaria that would come and go for the rest of his life.

The war was still affecting all our lives long after it ended. Pre-fabs were put up in the gaps on our street where houses had been lost to bomb damage. I got friendly with a boy called Billy whose family had moved in there. He was about my age and we went to the same school. He used to look out for me in the playground. Once a bee flew up the sleeve of my coat and, quick as a flash, Billy helped me get out of my coat, threw it on the ground and stamped on it to kill the bee before it could sting me.

Billy and I used to play together outside school too. We spent a lot of time playing on the street, as you could back then. We didn't have to worry about cars because nobody could afford to have one. We turned one of our neighbours' Anderson shelters into a den.

A gang of kids we knew would sometimes go to the site of the primary school that had been bombed. We weren't supposed to play on the bomb sites but many did.

I didn't go with Billy when he went to meet friends at the school so I don't know exactly what happened, but I do know that one day Billy fell from a wall and died from his injuries. Some of the children who were there that day said that he didn't fall. He was pushed.

After school, I went to work for the football pools, checking people's coupons, though I never checked a big winner. After work and at the weekends, I'd go to a local café, which is where I met my husband Tony, who was always by the jukebox because he loves music and is an excellent singer. Tony is obsessed with Burt Lancaster, so 'Burt' was his nickname, while mine was 'Jean' because I loved the actress Jean Simmons. We still call each other Burt and Jean today.

When I retired, I decided to look into my family history. I tried to find out about my father's war record. I knew he'd been in the First World War but couldn't find his name anywhere. Then I discovered that he was registered under 'Mawer' with an 'a' rather than Mower. It might have been a mistake but I wondered if he'd done it for a reason. I discovered later that he had a secret second family. I eventually met up with his sons from that family.

Investigating my family tree answered a lot of questions and not just about my dad. I knew that in 1951, when I was 12 and he was about 18, my brother Stan came into a sum of money, which had been left to him in the will of a nun called Sister Ethel. It was £100 which was quite a lot of money in those days, equivalent to around £4,500 now. At the time that it happened, I wasn't especially interested but years later I asked myself why Stan had come into that unexpected inheritance.

I recalled Mum telling me that a nun called Sister Ethel had asked to adopt my brother and that Mum had objected in the strongest possible terms but that was all I knew. Why would a nun have wanted to adopt Stan and where did she get the money she later left him? I was under the impression that nuns relinquished all their worldly goods upon entering Holy Orders. It didn't make sense. But by the time I started wondering about it, my parents and my brothers were all long gone and no-one else in the family knew anything about it.

I didn't think I would ever know the real story but around the year 2000, my husband was sorting through some boxes in the loft when he found a Bible belonging to my brother Leslie, which contained a dedication from the mysterious Sister Ethel. She had given it to Leslie as a gift on his 14th birthday in 1940. On the facing page was Leslie's name c/o Parrocks Lodge, Tatworth in Somerset. The date of the dedication set me thinking that this must be the place where Leslie and Stan had spent the war years.

With an address and a name to go on, I was able to work out that 'Sister Ethel' was Ethel Langdon. Her family, who were wealthy landowners, owned Parrocks Lodge, a beautiful Regency manor house, which looks like the sort of house you see in a Jane Austen adaptation. Sister Ethel was one of six siblings, none of whom had married, hence she'd inherited the estate.

I discovered that Sister Ethel, though a nun, had lived at Parrocks Lodge with a personal maid and other servants. She was a generous and caring lady who looked after the poor and less fortunate so it was obvious that she would rise to the challenge of taking in evacuees. One of those evacuees still lived in the village all those years later and he was able to tell me more. He sent me a photograph of five children – two boys and three girls – standing on the steps of Parrocks Lodge between an elegant woman in a white dress and patterned jacket and a nun in a severe black habit. I recognised my brothers at once.

Further investigations led me to a chap called Arthur, who had been evacuated with my brothers. He recalled life in Tatworth as very happy. He knew my brother Leslie well and had played alongside him in the Tatworth Evacuees Cricket Team. He'd also swapped his Meccano set for my brother Leslie's bike, in an exchange that became known as 'the big swap'. Apparently my mother wasn't too pleased about that.

I was very glad to find out that my brothers had had a happy evacuation. Sister Ethel was a Sister of the Society of Our Lady of Nazareth and a true humanitarian, who looked out for many people, including my little brother Stan, who had been left with a limp after getting ill. People were very kind to one another during the war. That's one of the good things that came out of it. The kindness some people showed and the life-long connections they made.

13

THE DEAD END KIDS

'We ain't sissies...'

THE CHILDREN OF BRITAIN WERE not entirely helpless during the Blitz. Many of them proved to be extraordinarily brave and resourceful. In Poplar in London's East End, a 17-year-old binman's son, Patsie Duggan, gathered together a gang of children who called themselves the 'Dead End Kids'. They co-opted the nickname given by the press to those children who had not been evacuated but stayed in the capital, occasionally making mischief as they tried to fill their days. During the first year of the war alone, the juvenile crime rate (crimes committed by children under the age of 14) rose by more than 40%.

But the Dead End Kids defied the low opinion of the media. They didn't spend the blacked-out nights stealing loot from bombed out houses, rather, they formed an unofficial rescue team, going out into the city night after night looking for people in need of assistance. Among their number was Patsie's younger sister, 13-year-old Maureen. Their youngest member and unofficial mascot was 10-year-old Shamus O'Brien, who was well known for his climbing skills.

Though they were only children, the Dead End Kids saved an impressive number of lives. Unhampered by an adult's sense of caution, they rushed into burning buildings armed only with the simple kit they'd been able to scrounge: ropes, spades and buckets of sand. Dead End Kid Ronnie Ayres became a local legend, after he rescued a pensioner from her burning house and carried her, still in her armchair, to the nearest shelter. On another occasion, the Dead End Kids saved 30 horses from a burning stable. The kids were said to have developed a method of roping incendiaries, as though roping cattle, before tossing them into the Thames. Most impressive of all, they helped 230 people get out of a damaged air-raid shelter, leading all of them to safety through a hail of bombs.

A newspaper article in *The Reading Eagle* of the time described the kids thus: 'a band of poorly dressed, grimy urchins who must now rank among the heroes of Britain... Through every kind of raid in all weathers, they have successfully fought the flames.

'They do not give a thought for falling shrapnel. They prefer to wear their caps at rakish angles instead of tin hats. When asked why they do not don tin helmets one of them replied: "We ain't sissies..."'

Alas, the Dead End Kids' spectacular daring came at a high cost. One night, when they were putting out incendiary bombs, Ronnie Ayres, then 18, and his 16-year-old friend Bert Eden were killed by a falling wall. The Dead End Kids' leader Patsie Duggan was badly injured in the same accident.

Just down the road in Stepney, 16-year-old Jimmy Cluff and three other boys had also volunteered to do fire-watching and rescue work on their street. One night, Jimmy's gang put out three fires and were on their way to see to a fourth when a high-explosive bomb stopped them in their tracks. Jimmy's three friends were killed but Jimmy was taken to Mile End Hospital, singing as he was carried there on a stretcher.

Jimmy Cluff underwent five operations and six blood transfusions but he still lost a leg and one eye.

'We don't know why he is alive,' his doctor told a newspaper. 'He just refuses to die.'

Jimmy's response was, 'They can't kill a kid from Stepney... They make us tough 'round here.' Then he observed that his left arm, which had been set in a cast at a right angle, might have looked like a Nazi salute, quipping, 'They've made me say "Heil Hitler" at last!'

Even younger children showed their mettle. Children like eight-year-old Michael McDermott who, frustrated by the air-raid debris littering the street he would usually play in, formed a mini demolition squad with his friends. Michael's crew, who donned tin hats to clear bricks from the road, included Peter, his little brother, aged four, and Benny and Bobby Few, aged five and three respectively. As the *Daily Mirror* reported at the time, 'Bobby Few, who is still sometimes wheeled in a pram, staggered along with two bricks in his hands.' Unfortunately for Michael, his mother was less impressed, telling the paper, 'Every time I need a shovel for the coal, I have to search for the children.'

Another little Londoner, Freddie Harrison was only six years old when he saved his two younger sisters, three-year-old Winifred Mary and 10-month-old Joy, from the ruins of their Blitzed home, digging them out of the rubble with his bare hands.

The story of Freddie's bravery became news worldwide, coming to the attention of a Canadian veteran, who sent little Freddie a letter of congratulations and a cheque for £4.15 (worth in the region of £200 now). The cheque and a model train engine were presented to Freddie by the Mayor of Hendon, at the Hendon Town Hall.

Like Freddie Harrison, the bravery of The Dead End Kids was eventually recognised by the authorities. They were invited to Downing Street to meet the prime minister. All was going well until one of the kids allegedly expressed his opinion on official recognition by loudly breaking wind in front of Churchill. To make matters worse, when the young farter was reprimanded by a civil servant, he snapped back, 'Why don't you just shut your ears, mister?'

After that, the breathless press coverage of the Dead End Kids' daring exploits began to die away. Even in wartime, the British public liked their heroes to have some manners.

14

CARRYING ON

The Scouts and Guides

PERHAPS THE DEAD END KIDS lacked fatherly guidance. Fortunately, a number of voluntary organisations were ready to fill the gap left behind when so many male role models - fathers, uncles and big brothers - were away at the war.

In 1939, the British people – men, women and children – had been issued with National Registration Cards, which contained their names, addresses and other information needed for administrative purposes. On the back of those cards issued to 16-year-olds was a reminder that they could and should be contributing to the war effort. The reminder said, 'Large numbers of boys and girls of your age are already giving up much of their spare time to different kinds of training or public service, as members of various organisations – whether clubs, Guides, Scouts or brigades, or helping in Civil Defence. Many boys too are preparing for future military service as members of the Cadets or Air Training Corps, or by serving now with the Home Guard... Some of you, of course, are still at school and your time is pretty well filled up. Your job is to get on with your education: your Headmaster or Headmistress will tell you if there is something more you might do. But it is the "bit extra" that counts and everyone in these days wants to do his utmost...'

The Scout Movement in particular came into its own, adopting the slogan, 'The Boy Scouts are carrying on'.

Even before the war started, the Scouts had helped to support refugees and displaced people. They welcomed Jewish children, evacuated from Nazi Germany and Austria under the Kindertransport Scheme. They also took part in Operation Pied Piper, organising groups of young evacuees for the journey to their new homes, providing valuable practical and moral support along the way.

In 1939, the Scouts were pressed into service to ready the country for the expected air raids. They helped people prepare their homes, providing teams to construct Morrison shelters, a table-like shelter that could be set up inside a house. Outside, they could be seen painting white lines along the edges of the roads to improve visibility in the blackouts.

When the Blitz arrived, the Scouts volunteered alongside the fire and ambulance and Air Raid Warden's Services, acting as couriers, stretcher bearers and fire watchers. They were trained in first aid. They worked alongside the Home Guard too. As the war went on, the Scouts had an important role in the 'Dig For Victory' campaign and joined the women of the Women's Timber Corp – the Lumber Jills – to help fell wood for telegraph poles and pit props.

The Scouts even played their part in the evacuation of Allied Troops from Dunkirk, with Sea Scouts crewing a number of motor boats that joined the flotilla of 'little ships' which bravely set out for France in May 1940.

The Girl Guides did their bit too. There were more than 750,000 Girl Guides in the UK in 1939. Having earned badges in all manner of skills, from first aid to telegraphy (a badge which required the holder to construct her own wireless receiver on which she could send Morse code at 30 letters per minute), the Guides, whose motto was 'Be Prepared', were more than ready for war.

They joined the Scouts in preparing the nation – painting kerbs and distributing gas masks. They worked in hospitals and evacuation centres too. In the countryside, the Guides collected sphagnum moss, which was used for healing wounds. They also collected rosehips, which they sold to the Ministry of Food to be made into vitamin-C syrup, to help keep the nation healthy.

The Guides were also given some more unusual tasks, such as collecting thousands of cotton reels. They weren't told why the cotton reels were needed but it was later revealed that they'd been gathered at the behest of top secret War Office department, MI9, Military Intelligence Section 9, which used the reels to hide microfilm and miniature maps to be passed to prisoners of war held in Germany.

Thanks to this important work, the Guides made such an impression that at the Lord Mayor's show in London in 1942, they received a salute from Churchill. But it was not always easy to carry on guiding during the war. In Japanese prison camps, all over the Far East, young scouts and guides risked a great deal to keep on meeting. Not least in the POW camp in Changi, in Singapore, where a group of exceptionally brave Girls Guides, including nine-year-old Olga Henderson, held clandestine meetings to make a very special quilt.

Olga Henderson, 95

I WAS BORN IN SINGAPORE. My parents were both British ex-pats, who had come to the Far East for work, but I grew up among children of all nationalities and was fluent in Malay. I'd go with my mother to the market and translate what the stall-keepers told her. Our friends and neighbours came from every country and faith and we celebrated religious holidays as a village. We marked Diwali and Hari Raya (the Malay name for Eid), which was my favourite festival. Every house was decorated with tiny oil lamps and there were firecrackers for the children.

We heard about the war in Europe when it started but it seemed very far away. We carried on living a very normal life right up until the beginning of 1942. We spent Christmas 1941 as usual, hosting a big Boxing Day party at our house, and at New Year we went to our hut on Changi Beach in Singapore for a little holiday. When we left to go back home, I was in a terrible mood, knowing we had to go back to school the next day. My younger brother Peter was more excited because he was going to school for the first time but he didn't have long to learn the ropes because just a couple of weeks after term began, the school was closed for the war.

I didn't know that while we'd been having our usual Christmas, the Japanese had been capturing British colonies all over the Far East. As far as I was concerned, I was just happy I didn't have to go to school.

A couple of weeks later, my brothers and I were playing with our guinea pigs on the verandah when we heard the sound of heavy boots coming up the staircase outside. When we looked we saw an army truck and, sure enough, our visitor turned out to be a soldier.

Dad answered the door. We heard the soldier tell him we were being evacuated. The Japanese were not far from our village and we had to go across the causeway to Singapore. When Dad asked how long we had to get ready, the answer came back, 'Half an hour.'

While Mum and Dad packed clothes and food, we children packed our toys. It was like a game to us, as we rushed around the house. George wanted to bring a toy lorry he'd been given for Christmas. I packed my 'Betsy Wetsy' doll and her wardrobe full of tiny clothes. Peter had a couple of pet chickens. He wanted to bring them along. The chickens and our toys were loaded onto the truck.

As we waved goodbye to our house, it felt as though we were off on an adventure. Singapore to us then was the place we went to enjoy ourselves. When Dad had a day off work, we would often go into the city to shop and see a film. Just a couple of weeks before, we'd been to the city to see Mum's Japanese tailor, who was making her a new dress. I loved going with Mum to see her tailor. His wife would always make us something to eat and we counted his children as friends. The memory of all those exciting outings was in my head as we drove towards the causeway that day in January 1942.

When we got there, a group of British soldiers was waiting for us, keen for us to hurry up because their instructions were to blow up the causeway the moment we were across. We were the last European family to be evacuated. Dad knew the causeway well. He'd been involved in building the customs house to the side of it. While the border officers checked our vehicle, Dad went to see what the soldiers were planning. He could see at once that the charges they'd set were in the wrong place and wouldn't get the job done. But the soldiers weren't interested in Dad's opinion. They were just following orders. Dad left them to it but he wasn't wrong. They didn't blow the bridge up properly and you could still easily get across, as the Japanese would not long after.

Singapore was very different from the last time we'd been there. The island was full of Allied troops. There were soldiers camping on the green in front of our uncle Tom's house, where we were staying. The soldiers were fascinating to us children and kind too, sharing their rations while they waited to be sent to the front line.

It was a strange time. We'd always loved visiting Uncle Tom. He had an elderly Malay housekeeper who spoiled us rotten. Being *evacuated* to Uncle Tom's house was very different. Though Uncle Tom's housekeeper did her best, food was limited. We had to kill one of Peter's pet chickens. There wasn't much space and we had to sleep with mattresses on top of us, to protect us from shrapnel as the Japanese were continually bombing and there were no air raid shelters nearby. It was all we could do to stay safe.

I'll never forget the morning the soldiers camping on the green went off to fight. My brothers and I watched them go from Uncle Tom's front gate. One soldier saw my red, white and blue hair ribbon and asked if he could have it for luck. I handed it over right away and he tied it to his kit bag.

While this was going on, Mum and Dad decided it was time for us to leave the island. Mum took us down to Keppel Harbour, where the Allies were loading expats onto ships bound for Australia and South Africa. It was chaos. Thousands of people were trying to get away. It was everyone for themselves. When we got onto the gangplank of a ship at last, I thought we were on our way, but when Mum handed over our documents, the man in charge told her we weren't on his list. We weren't in Singapore on British government business, therefore we weren't his responsibility. He sent us away.

It didn't feel like it at the time but that man probably saved our lives. While Mum tried to work out what to do, Peter and I stood on the harbour's edge and waved to a ship that was setting off, carrying some children we knew. We waved as though they were off on holiday, not trying to escape a war. But the minute the ship was out of the harbour, two Japanese fighter planes flew low over the ship and shot at the people on deck.

Mum quickly pulled us away from the danger, into one of the storm drains that criss-crossed the city, thinking it would be safer than staying on the streets. I'll never forget the sight that greeted us down there. The water running through the drains that day was bright red with the blood of people dying up above. I don't know how we kept going.

We made it back to Uncle Tom's house but everything had changed. There was no food and no water either, as the Japanese had bombed the water supply. And though they had outnumbered the Japanese troops, the Allies were outflanked. On February 15th 1942, the Allies capitulated and all Europeans – like my family – were immediately declared 'enemy aliens'.

Not long after, a Japanese officer arrived at the house to tell us we had to register at Singapore's courthouse. From there, we were sent to Katong, where the women and children were separated from the men. We had to say 'goodbye' to Dad.

The walk to Katong took us across a bridge decorated with the severed heads of various men, including some Chinese, who had tried to help the Allies hold off the invasion. The Japanese had stuck their heads on spikes. Mum tried to keep us from looking at them but I only needed to see them for a minute for their faces to be in my head for the rest of my life. I will never forget those poor men.

We were in Katong for about three weeks, while the Japanese decided what to do with us. The answer was to send us to Changi Prison. The newly finished prison had been built by the British to hold 600. The prisoners were released to make way for three times that number of internees.

My family – me, Mum, my older sister Mary and my two little brothers, Peter and George – was allocated a cell, which we had to share with another woman. The cell was originally designed for two adult men. It had a latrine in one corner, which was always overflowing. The only window was set so high in the wall we couldn't see out of it and the beds were concrete plinths that couldn't be moved to make more space. There was no bedding.

This was to be home for the next two years.

I think that being interned was harder for the adult women than it was for us children. We made the most of having ready-made playmates in the camp. We had some schooling and we would often put on little plays. One of the women – Mrs Ennis – set up a guide group. We weren't meant to meet in groups – the Japanese were paranoid it would give us the opportunity to plan to escape – so we had to be very secretive about it, but we did what guides in the outside world did. We said the oath and worked towards earning badges, which we made ourselves out of any scraps of fabric we could find.

Mrs Ennis's birthday was coming up and we guides decided that we wanted to make her a quilt as a gift. We gathered as many scraps of fabric as we could find with the idea that each of us would sew a 'flower' of so many patches that could be joined together. At the centre of each flower was a black hexagon, on which would be embroidered the name of the girl who had made it. I remember that the black fabric was salvaged from a pair of worn-out trousers given to us by a Japanese woman, who was in the camp because she was married to a European.

Once or twice, I was sewing my flower when someone spotted a guard coming near. When that happened, I would tuck my sewing, needles and all, up the leg of my knickers, where the elastic held it in place. I sensed the danger of being caught.

After we made our quilt, the adult women made a couple of quilts too. They very cleverly made the first one for the camp's Japanese commandant. Pleased with the gift, which he must have thought showed he had the internees' respect, he let the women make a second quilt for the men's camp. What he didn't know was that they embroidered it with secret messages for their loved ones on the other side of the wall.

Later in the war the Japanese decided they wanted to move civilian prisoners out of Changi so that they could keep military PoWs there instead. After a series of successful sabotage attacks on the Japanese by the Allies, they were afraid there would be an uprising. We women and children and the civilian men were moved to a former RAF camp at Sime Road. It was awful. The buildings where they expected us to sleep were half falling down. There were 118 of us in a hut built for 34 with only one toilet.

As the war went on, the Japanese treated us more harshly. We were all put to work – used as slave labour. We were hungry all the time but we weren't allowed to eat the food we grew. That was for the guards. My brother Peter was barbarically whipped for picking up a jambu fruit that had fallen from a tree.

We were so hungry. Food was constantly in our thoughts. A leaf of spinach would have been regarded as gold.

It felt like the end of the war would never come. It was constantly thought of and talked about. The speculation became an obsession for some. For others, it was just about getting through each day. We saw the Allied planes flying overhead but never dared to think that we might be winning. Even if the Allies did win, it might not be good news for us prisoners. In 1945, now aged 13, I was part of a group of women that was given the job of digging a tunnel in the hillside. We were told it was for storing supplies but after we were liberated, the Allies found papers in the Japanese Commandants' office with instructions that we prisoners were to be herded into that tunnel and blown up. The date was set for September. Thank goodness we were liberated a month earlier.

After the war, we couldn't go back to our home. It had been looted. Instead, we were put on a ship bound for Southampton. I suppose we were excited. My siblings and I had never been to England before. When we arrived after a long journey, we went to stay with some of Mum's relatives. It was hard to get used to how grey and cold everything was. Although we'd been issued with coupons and ration books, we didn't have any money to buy anything. We'd lost everything in Malaya.

Eventually, Dad decided that he couldn't stay in England and he got a job back in Malaysia. My big sister Mary stayed in the UK to train as a nurse, but I was very happy to go back to Johor Bahru, which always felt like home to me. I met my husband Jim not long after we got back. Like us, he'd been in a camp during the war. He'd had a horrific time in Labuan Camp in Borneo. Because we had that shared experience, he and I understood each other. We had many wonderful years together, travelling all over the world and raising four children. Sadly, I lost him early due to the effects the treatment and suffering he'd experienced in camp had on his health.

The quilt we Changi guides made is in the Imperial War Museum now, where it is kept in a special temperature-controlled archive, in a glass case to protect it from damage. Before it can be uncovered, the museum staff have to check the temperature and level of light in the room.

It takes me right back to see those carefully embroidered flowers. When I read my old friends' names, I remember what it was like all those years ago in camp, when being part of that girl guide group meant so much. I'll never forget the other girls who were at Changi and Sime Road with me. I hope one day to find out what happened to my friend Ossie Hancock, who was one of the 'three muske-teers' with me and Eileen Harris. Sometimes I think that the world has forgotten us - the child internees and people like my mother, whose bravery kept us alive through that terrible time. There were no medals for the likes of us, you see.

15

THE FRIENDLY INVASION

America Joins The War

AFTER THE FALL OF PARIS in the summer of 1940, Britain was isolated in the fight against Hitler's Germany. On the European mainland, Poland, Denmark, Norway, Belgium, the Netherlands, Luxembourg, Yugoslavia and Greece had all fallen under Nazi occupation. It was widely expected that the British Isles would be next but the United States remained stubbornly neutral while the British faced the terror of the Blitz.

In September 1940, Germany, Italy and Japan signed the Tripartite Pact, a defensive military alliance. Under the pact, Japan recognised Germany and Italy's right to establish a 'new order' in Europe. In reciprocation, Germany and Italy recognised Japan's right to expand its own territory in Greater East Asia.

The Tripartite Act would change everything. Confident that their actions would face no opposition from Hitler or Mussolini, the Japanese were emboldened to bomb the US naval base in Hawaii's Pearl Harbor.

The surprise attack on December 7th 1941 saw the US lose four battleships, while four more were badly damaged. In excess of 2,400 military personnel and civilians were killed that day, with a further 1,000 wounded. Suddenly the United States could no longer afford to remain on the fence in the war against Hitler and the Axis powers and, in January of the following year, the first American servicemen began to arrive in the UK to prepare for the pushback in Europe.

To the people of Britain, who had already lived through two and a half years of blitzes and shortages, the GIs (which stands for 'Government Issue', stamped all over their equipment, stores and clothing) brought a welcome shot of glamour to the endless grey days and blacked out nights. Their arrival in early 1942 was dubbed 'the friendly invasion' as the GIs quickly ingratiated themselves with their hosts. Before arriving in the UK the GIs had received instruction in how to behave around the British, in the form of a small cultural guide containing such useful advice as, 'The British don't know how to make a good cup of coffee. You don't know how to make a good cup of tea. It's an even swap,' and 'Don't make fun of British speech or accents. You sound just as funny to them.'

Whether or not they sounded funny, the GIs had their pick of the young British women. Not least because they earned five times more than the average British soldier, something else which was noted in the cultural guide. 'You are higher paid than the "British Tommy". Don't rub it in.'

However, not all GIs were equal. At least, not within their own ranks.

Of the three million GIs who passed through the UK on their way to fight in Europe, around 240,000 (eight percent) were African American. By the time the GIs arrived in Britain, the American Civil War, which had pitted the northern states against the southern Confederate States of America over the subject of slavery, had been finished for almost 80 years, but in the 1940s the United States was still a divided nation when it came to race. Those divisions persisted within the US forces. Even while serving overseas, white and Black GIs dined in separate messes and had separate social lives, according to the racial segregation laws – the Jim Crow laws of the Southern United States – that kept them apart back home.

When the US joined the war, it was assumed by the US top brass that the race laws which prevailed on their bases in the UK would be applied to their men outside the bases too. But they reckoned without the British public. While undoubtedly racial prejudice existed in the United Kingdom, there were no segregation laws and the Black American soldiers found themselves largely welcome when they socialised off-base in the British pubs and dance halls. In Cambridge, when the US Army tried to impose a colour bar outside one of their bases, a British landlord put up a sign saying 'Black Troops Only'.

Some white GIs, especially those from the Southern States were infuriated to see their Black comrades mixing with the locals and there were a number of terrible violent clashes between white and Black US servicemen, the most famous of which was 'The Battle of Bamber Bridge', which took place at Ye Olde Hob Inn, at Bamber Bridge in Lancashire on June 24th 1943. The incident began when two white US military policemen tried to arrest Private Eugene Nunn, a Black soldier of the 1511th Quartermaster Truck Regiment, who was drinking after hours in the pub with British locals. Staff Sergeant William Byrd, who was also Black, was initially able to defuse the situation but as the MPs drove away from the pub, a bottle was thrown at their jeep. The MPs returned with reinforcements and confronted the Black soldiers as they walked back to their base. During the confrontation, shots were fired and Black soldier Private William Crossland was killed when a bullet hit him in the back.

A five-hour long firefight ensued, leaving seven more wounded. In the aftermath, a court martial convicted 32 Black soldiers of mutiny. Though the same court martial found that racist attitudes and poor discipline among the MPs was the catalyst for the violence, none of the white MPs, including the one who killed Crossland, were charged.

Despite the horrendous tensions within the US forces, British women met and happily fell in love with Black GIs. However, a US soldier could not take a wife without the permission of his commanding officer. To the white GIs, this was hardly an obstacle. Over the course of the war, more than 60,000 British women became 'GI brides'. But it's significant that not one of the corresponding GI grooms was Black.

While 30 of the 50 American states still had laws prohibiting 'miscegenation' – sexual relationships and marriage between people of different races – no white US Army officer could ever give permission for one of his Black soldiers to marry a white woman, given that their marriage would be illegal back home. The insistence on upholding segregation laws, had horrible repercussions for the children of these unions.

Nearly half of the babies born to white British mothers and Black GIs were given up to the local authorities because their families were unable to cope with the complications around raising a mixed-race child outside marriage. Many of the mothers who gave up their babies hoped they might be adopted by loving families but it was hard to find British families who were willing to take the children on.

An obvious solution, that the children be sent to join their extended families in the United States was stymied by the fact that, as far as British law was concerned, their Black GI fathers were not considered to be next of kin, because they were not named on the children's birth certificates. They were putative fathers only. The proposal hit another road block in the 1939 Adoption Act, which ruled that British children could only be sent abroad to be adopted by British families. What this meant was the children who might have been raised in loving families ended up growing up in children's homes.

16

TO THE MANOR BORN...

The Brocket Babies

ILLEGITIMACY STILL CARRIED AN ENORMOUS stigma during the war. Even when London's maternity hospitals were evacuated to the countryside, social mores dictated that single mothers-to-be were kept separate from their married sisters.

There were two types of unmarried mother at Brocket Hall, a requisitioned stately home turned wartime maternity hospital: those who had money and those who did not. The treatment they received differed accordingly. Those women who could pay their way (either because they were from well-to-do families or had been knocked up by a man who was) were able to rest before and after giving birth at Lemsford House, which was once the vicarage for the church of St John The Evangelist on the Brocket Estate. Those who didn't have money had to work for their keep. Never mind that they were heavily pregnant.

Unmarried women without means slept in the attic at Brocket Hall and worked as cleaners or cooks in the maternity hospital, sometimes skivvying right up until they went into labour. These unfortunate women wore brown uniforms to distinguish them from the respectable mums-to-be, and their babies, when they were born, were nicknamed 'brownies'.

Just as their mothers had been kept separate for propriety's sake, the brownies, who were usually earmarked for adoption before they were even born, were kept separate from those infants born into 'wedlock'. The brownies' mothers were not allowed to see or hold them except to feed them at strictly timetabled intervals. It was a regime intended to prevent bonding before the babies were handed over to 'decent' adoptive families, and their mothers returned home and tried to pretend that they'd never given birth at all. That might as well have been the case. Records pertaining to the adoptions were sporadic and many of the Brocket Brownies would never know the circumstances of their birth.

Ironically, Brocket Hall was a place quite used to scandal. During the early years of Queen Victoria's reign, Brocket Hall's chatelaine was Lady Caroline Lamb, mistress of the notorious Lord Byron. When Lady Caroline threw a banquet in honour of her husband Lord Melbourne, she served herself naked in a soup tureen. Lord Melbourne's successor, prime minister Lord Palmerston, is said to have expired on Brocket Hall's billiard table. He was underneath a housemaid at the time.

In the late 1930s, Brocket Hall belonged to another aristocrat of questionable character. The second Lord Brocket, Arthur Ronald Nall-Cain, was a Nazi sympathizer, who attended Adolf Hitler's 50th birthday party. So close was Nall-Cain to Hitler's Foreign Minister, Joachim von Ribbentrop, that one of the guest suites at Brocket Hall was named the 'Von Ribbentrop Room'. Thus it's unlikely that the second Lord Brocket would have predicted the next phase in his grand estate's story. In 1939, Brocket Hall was transformed into a 50-bed maternity hospital for London's evacuated mothers-to-be. Nall-Cain, meanwhile, was interned on the Isle of Man.

The first baby to be born in the new maternity hospital was Alan Lowe, who arrived on September 3rd 1939, the very day Britain declared war on Germany. Among the 8,000 or so 'Brocket Babies' who came after him were film director Mike Leigh, novelist Jim Crace, BBC presenter Colin Berry and war baby Vertrelia 'Bunny' Taylor, whose father Robert was a Black GI.

Bunny Taylor, 82

I JUST GOT MY BROCKET birth certificate. We've got a club and we have reunions. I've been back to the house a couple of times as an adult. It's a conference centre and hotel now. My best friend from school took me there for lunch on my birthday a few years ago. It was lovely to go back and see where I was born.

My family comes from Waltham Forest in North East London. When the war broke out, my mum Adele and my two uncles were still living at home. Mum was 20 and she was working as a shorthand typist. When the GIs arrived, my grandparents agreed to have one of them billeted in the house. That was my dad, Robert Taylor from Illinois.

The whole family loved Robert at once. He came bearing gifts they could only dream of while everything was 'on the ration'. He had lovely manners too. He was really old-fashioned and was always ready to help out if needed. My grandma adored him. She treated him like an extra son. So did my grandfather. Everybody thought he was wonderful. All the same, I don't think my grandparents ever thought that their daughter would fall in love with him. After all, he was Black.

I don't think the people of Waltham Forest were bothered about having Black soldiers around. Most people were just glad to see them. They were just as willing to lay down their lives for us as the white blokes were, after all. But when Mum got pregnant, it was a bit of a problem.

Mum had a good job but she still depended on her parents for a roof over her head. They didn't like the idea that their daughter could have a child out of wedlock but my mum and dad couldn't get married even if they wanted to. Because he was a US soldier, my dad couldn't take a wife without the permission of his commanding officer. Black soldiers were never given permission to marry white British women because of the way the law worked back in America.

Dad described himself as having Blackfoot ancestry, meaning he belonged to the Blackfoot Confederacy of indigenous North American tribes, but the miscegenation laws applied to Native American soldiers too. If my dad had tried to go against orders and married Mum anyway, he'd have found himself in jail.

My grandparents decided the best thing to do was try to keep Mum's pregnancy a secret. When they couldn't keep it secret anymore, Mum went to the mother and baby home at Brocket Hall.

Because she and my dad had money, they could afford to pay for Mum's board and she didn't have to work while she was waiting to go into labour. When the time came for me to arrive, she was taken to the main house, to Lord Melbourne's bedroom, which was set up as the birthing suite. That's where I was born.

I know lots of babies born at Brocket Hall were given up for adoption but Mum was always going to bring me home and my dad was there to meet her when she did. They had their first argument over what to call me.

Dad wanted to call me Roberta, after himself, but Mum wasn't having that. Instead, I ended up being called Vertrelia, a family name on Dad's side. I was christened Vertrelia in the church – St John's – on the Brocket Estate. But Vertrelia was too grand a name for a little baby. Soon everyone started calling me Bobby, after Dad. Then a doctor called me Bunny. It was Bunny that stuck. I don't think I even knew I actually had another name until I went to school.

I wasn't the only one who had a change of name in those early days. Mum couldn't become Mrs Taylor by marriage but she changed her surname to Taylor by deed poll, so that she could have the same name as Dad and me.

A year after I was born, Dad was one of the thousands of US soldiers sent to the Normandy beaches on D-Day. Mum and I stayed in Waltham Forest with my grandparents. Then when I was about 18 months old, while Dad was still away, Mum got ill. She was diagnosed with 'Pott's disease', tuberculosis of the spine, which can damage your vertebrae and even lead to paralysis.

There were only two treatment options available for spinal TB back then. The first was to have a metal rod fitted in your back. It required only a short hospital stay but it meant you were left with no flexibility. You were ram-rod straight the whole time. Mum had seen other TB patients who'd gone down that route and couldn't imagine a lifetime of not ever being able to bend over to pick me up. Mind you, the second option was no less drastic: complete bed rest on a plaster bed for months, or even years, on end.

Mum picked the bed rest at Waltham Abbey Isolation Hospital because she knew I would be safe with my grandparents and uncles.

I wasn't able to see much of Mum while she was ill because of the risk of infection but they were good years. My grandmother was very loving. My grandfather was kind too, though he seemed to spend most of his time reading the newspaper in the corner of the room. Mum's younger brothers, my uncles, treated me like I was their little pet. They were always taking me out and about with them. On his way to work in the morning, my uncle Terry would sit me on the seat of his motorbike and give me a ride to the top of our road, where I'd jump off and run back home. I loved being the youngest in the family. It was a wonderful time.

Dad survived landing on the beaches on D-Day and fought on into Germany, where he took a bullet in the leg. He was sent back to England to recover so I got to see a lot of him then. At the end of the war, he had to go home to America but he kept writing to Mum and me and sending money for my upkeep. Mum was still in hospital when I turned four and started school.

I really liked school and I was a good student. I was near the top of the class and I had a lot of friends. But suddenly, when I was about six, everything changed. I was sent away to boarding school in Somerset. At least that's what I was told it was. A boarding school.

The place was run by a woman called Taki. She was a ballerina but she'd had to give up dancing after she had an accident, so she'd bought this big farm in the countryside and started selling it to parents like it was a private school. There was a uniform, with a cloak, so we looked the part when our families dropped us off. I'm sure they thought they were doing the best for us. But as soon as they were out of sight, everything was different. It wasn't like Harry Potter, that's for sure. The cloaks came off and so did the pretence.

We didn't get many lessons. Occasionally, Taki would teach us a bit of ballet or Latin or French, so we'd have something to tell our families about I suppose, but most of the time we seemed to be working around the farm as unpaid labour.

Every single morning we were up at the crack of dawn – even the little ones – collecting eggs and cleaning out the animals. There were cows and horses to be seen to every day. Through the autumn and winter we had to pick sugar beet. We plucked chickens. I hated doing that. We all did. We were only little kids but that didn't seem to matter to Taki. We just had to do as we were told. We had to muck in. What else could we do? We couldn't call our parents to tell them what was happening. If we wrote a letter, Taki would know what it said. And we were miles away from home. If we ran away, where would we go? It was a very different life from the one I'd been used to.

At primary school in Waltham Forest, I don't remember anyone really commenting about my colour. Nobody seemed that bothered. All that changed in Somerset. Suddenly, I was really aware that I didn't look the same as everybody else. As well as Taki, there were a number of local women at the farm who were supposed to be looking after us and they were horrible.

These women had never seen a Black child before. They decided that they didn't know what to do with my curly hair and they couldn't be bothered to learn, so they let it go wild. Once, one of them picked me up by the ankles and pretended to wash the floor with my hair, as if I was a mop. They thought that was a great joke.

It was never the kids who made the comments. The other children were alright. I made some friends. We all looked out for each other.

There were some happy times in Somerset, mostly when we kids were left to our own devices. It was an outdoorsy sort of existence and when we weren't working, I enjoyed that. I did learn to ride a horse. We didn't have formal lessons or anything like that, but when we were mucking them out we'd sometimes jump on and take them round the fields. We didn't have saddles or reins. We just clung on to their necks somehow. Once, when I was on the back of one of the horses, one of the farm hands slapped it on the backside and it raced off with me hanging on for dear life. I came off of course and was knocked out when I landed on the hard ground.

One day, we were out in the fields and a farm worker called Anthea was driving a tractor, pulling a sort of roller behind it. We children would sit on the bar above that roller for a ride. Every so often, one of us would run back to the farmhouse to find out the time. When it was my turn, I ran to the farmhouse and back again as fast as I could. I was trying to get back on top of the roller when I slipped underneath it.

I don't know how it happened. All the other kids screamed for Anthea to stop and she did, just as the roller got up to my pelvis. The ground was soft underneath, which probably saved by life, and I might have got away without too much damage but for some reason, rather than get everyone together to lift the roller straight off me, Anthea decided that the best way to get me out from underneath was to keep driving so that the roller went right over my body, breaking my back. I thought I was going to die. I don't know how I didn't.

I spent the next week in hospital. I was in a lot of pain but some of the nurses were far from sympathetic. To keep us warm at night, the children on my ward were given hot water bottles, which were removed from the bed after we fell asleep to avoid any accidents with spills. When my grandmother used to take the hot water bottle away at home, she would do it carefully, without waking me up, but the nurses would just rip back the sheets and leave us shivering. They would laugh at me as I tried to keep warm by huddling at the bottom of the bed. I was their entertainment. They picked on me much more than the others. They'd never seen a kid like me before.

No-one from my family visited because Taki didn't tell them what had happened. When I was well enough to be discharged, I was taken straight back to school and went to work in the farmyard again. I was still in pain. My back gives me trouble to this day.

I spent three years in Somerset in all, never going home for the holidays. Even when Mum was discharged from the isolation hospital and moved back in with my grandparents, I stayed with Taki at her school. When I finally went back to Waltham Forest one summer, I didn't take much with me, because I didn't think I would be staying long, but Mum took me for a walk and she took me by the hand and said, 'Would you like to go to Selwyn in September?'

Selwyn was the local junior school I'd been at before I was sent away. I said, 'Yes' and that was that. I never went back to the farm, not even to fetch my things. They didn't send them to Essex after me. Not even the little pair of cowboy boots that my dad had sent to me from America. I loved those boots.

The farm was never mentioned again. I was nine years old by now and my three years in Somerset had left me behind the children who'd stayed at Selwyn all that time. I was left out socially too. I couldn't fit back into the old gang.

Why was I sent away? For a long time, I assumed it was because Mum was in hospital and my grandparents felt too old and tired to be bringing up a six-year-old. But decades later, Uncle Terry told me what he thought had happened. He said that my grandfather was getting into politics – he was on the local council – and some of his constituents were unhappy with the idea that he had a Black grandchild.

Even after the Black GIs had done so much for us during the war. The easiest thing to do was to send me away so that it wouldn't be an issue. Out of sight, out of mind. I couldn't believe it. I'd never thought that my grandfather might be embarrassed by my colour. I still don't believe it but I suppose it makes sense.

All the time I was in Somerset, my dad had continued to write to Mum and send money for my upkeep. Now that I was old enough to read a letter for myself, he started to write directly to me too. He sent me presents that made me the envy of my school friends. I had Levi's jeans long before anyone else did.

My dad wasn't the only one from my American family who wanted to keep in touch. His mum, my grandmother, also wrote. She could hardly see and her writing would go off the end of the page. It took me ages to decipher those letters but I loved getting them and I kept them for years. I had a picture of her and I remember looking at a book of photographs of Native American women and deciding that my grandmother might be Sioux from the shape of her face.

I always hoped that one day I would visit my father in America and meet my wider family but it didn't ever happen. When I was about 16, Mum announced that she was going to get married. She wrote to my dad, telling him what was happening and he wrote back, telling her that he would not write again unless she wanted him to. He wanted to respect her status as another man's wife. In a letter to me, he said that he wanted to continue writing to me but would understand if I didn't want that now that I had a stepfather.

Of course I still wanted to be in contact with my dad but I didn't get the chance to make that decision because I didn't know it was a possibility. Mum didn't actually show me the letter, she just told me that Dad had written to her saying he didn't want to be in touch with either of us anymore. I thought he'd abandoned me. I suppose Mum just wanted him out of her life. It was less complicated for her that way.

I finished school and trained to be a nursery nurse but I wanted to see more of the world. That's why I joined the Women's Royal Naval Service. I was given a role in the uniform department, making sure everyone was properly kitted out. I was one of only three black women that I knew of in the WRNS at that time and one of those women was my boss.

I felt like I had found a new family in the WRNS, one where I could be myself. It wasn't legal to be gay in the armed forces in those days but there was a group of lesbians – the gay girls – who would get together. We had to be very careful though. You couldn't be openly out.

When I left the Wrens, I found work as an ambulance driver and when that got too tough for me with my back problems – we had to lift some very heavy people – I became a bus driver instead. I liked that job. You'd get to know your passengers and sometimes they would bring me little presents.

Over the years, I kept in touch with some of my Wren friends and became a flag-bearer for Remembrance Sunday. I still visit other former Wrens on behalf of the WRNS Benevolent Trust and among them are some World War Two veterans. The WRNS has given me a great sense of community and even brought me the love of my life. She and I met at a memorial service for a World War Two Wren. We sat next to each other in the church and that was that.

I'd love to know what happened to my father but after he stopped writing, I completely lost track of him. I heard that he went into politics in the US. Perhaps one day I'll take a DNA test. I'd like to know more about my ancestry on that side. These things feel more important as the years go by.

17

A FAMILY TORN APART BY THE HOLOCAUST

*'The war is still impacting
on our lives...'*

AS THE CHILDREN OF THE Kindertransport knew, Hitler intended to wipe out the Jewish people but it was not until December 17th 1942 that the UK Parliament officially recognised the Holocaust. On that day, foreign secretary Anthony Eden told MPs that he had received 'reliable reports... regarding the barbarous and inhuman treatment to which Jews are being subjected in German-occupied Europe.'

He continued, 'The able-bodied are slowly worked to death in labour camps. The infirm are left to die of exposure and starvation or are deliberately massacred in mass executions. The number of victims of these bloody cruelties is reckoned in many hundreds of thousands of entirely innocent men, women and children.'

Eden's words astonished the assembled MPs, who bombarded him with questions as to what should be done. Eventually, the MPs did the only thing they could do in that moment. They stood for a minute of silence, requested by Labour MP William Cluse.

In the two and a half further years it would take for the Allies to defeat Nazi Germany, many millions of Jewish people lost their lives. For those Jews who escaped to Britain, news of the suffering of those they'd had to leave behind was especially hard to bear, becoming a burden they would struggle not to pass on to their children.

Jackie Kershaw, whose mother Edith was a Jewish refugee, explains how the Holocaust cast a shadow over her quintessential English childhood.

Jackie Kershaw, 84

MY MOTHER EDITH CAME FROM Vienna in Austria. She was part of a large Jewish family who all lived in the same apartment building in the Jewish quarter of the city. Though they weren't rich, they lived a lovely genteel sort of life and even had a housemaid. They were very cultured. My mother loved to go to the opera. She couldn't afford good seats so she would either sit right at the top of the opera house or even stand up, just so she could hear the music. She and my grandmother loved to go to the coffee houses too.

My grandfather was a salesman, specialising in woollen underwear which was very important because it got so cold in the Viennese winters. Meanwhile, my grandmother had a linen shop and even made a trousseau for a Bulgarian princess. My mother trained to be a milliner and married a businessman called Richard Krochmalnik.

When the political landscape in Austria started to change, Richard decided to go to the United States. I assume the plan was that my mother would follow him sooner or later, but she didn't. She stayed on in Vienna with her family. Things didn't get better. She often told me about the Anschluss; how they went to bed on the evening of March 11th 1938 and woke up the following morning to discover that everything was unutterably changed. Vienna as my family knew it had disappeared overnight. There were Nazi flags waving from all the official buildings and the streets were suddenly full of men in uniform. It was a complete and terrible transformation.

That same day, the local chief of police, who was friends with my grandmother, came to warn her that the Nazis were planning to round up their enemies, starting with the communists. Her son, my uncle Arthur, was a communist. On the advice of the police chief, Uncle Arthur and my grandfather left Vienna that very day.

When they got to Poland, my grandfather told Uncle Arthur that he would have to go on alone because my grandfather worried that he would be a burden. Arthur went on to Sweden, where he was arrested and sent back. That happened three times before the Jewish community in Sweden stepped in and said they would support him to ensure he wasn't a burden on the state. After that he was allowed to stay. He was able to get work as a furrier and eventually took over the business that had employed him. He met his wife Orla and lived in Sweden for the rest of his life.

With my uncle and grandfather gone, life was quickly changing for the worse for the rest of my family in Vienna. Many Austrians were embracing the Nazification of the city and making life increasingly uncomfortable for their Jewish neighbours. Yet still my grandmother would not leave. For my mother, the final straw came when she and some of her friends were forced to get down on their hands and knees and scrub the streets. When she had finished, my mother asked a Nazi officer, 'Can I have a certificate to prove that I've done my duty?' In response, the officer slapped her across the face. That was the moment when Mum decided she had to go.

She applied to an agency that was finding work for people in England. At that time, you could only get into England as a domestic servant. She was matched with a Mrs Owtram, who was looking for help at her father-in-law's house Newland Hall near Lancaster. Mrs Owtram – Bunty – wrote the necessary letters promising employment and my mother was on her way. Her journey across Europe was not easy and she didn't like to talk about it.

Mum didn't speak a word of English but she told me that she found the British people very kind. When she arrived, she showed the taxi driver her address for the night – the YWCA. He took her there and insisted on collecting her the following morning to take her to the station and make sure she got the right train for her onward journey to Lancaster. She never forgot that.

My mother thought that Newland Hall, the Owtram family's house, was very strange. It was such a completely different way of life to what she had been used to. But she did settle down. She became very friendly with the cook, who gave her lots of recipes. I think the cook had once worked for Queen Mary. As a result, my mother made the best Christmas pudding you have ever tasted but she never shared the recipe. Not even with me.

She told me that right before the war, the Owtrams threw a fancy-dress party and one of the guests dressed up as Hitler. My mother was so incensed that she refused to come downstairs while this guest was in the house. Colonel Owtram – or perhaps it was his wife – made the guest go upstairs to see my mother and apologise.

Even after Mum had left, my grandmother and aunt didn't want to leave Vienna but eventually they were persuaded to go to Belgium to stay with my grandmother's sisters. They thought they would be safe there but outside the family, people wouldn't speak to them. Everyone was afraid. When war broke out, my mother finally convinced her sister and my grandmother that they must come to the UK before it was too late.

One of my grandmother's sisters – a very beautiful woman, much younger than the rest – was caught in a round-up of Jews after

Belgium was occupied. While they were being kept in a holding cell, one of the men had a heart attack. The officer in charge said to my grandmother's sister, 'Go and get a doctor.' I think that because she was so beautiful, he was trying to save her by giving her the opportunity to run away. But she wouldn't go. She told the officer, 'I'm not going to do what you tell me.' Of course, we never heard from her again. Other people who had been there that day told us what happened.

With the help of Mrs Owtram, Mum got my grandmother and her sister both jobs near Lancaster in a big house which belonged, I think, to the Duke of Devonshire. My aunt, who had been made a parlour maid, recalled being asked to hoover one of the rooms, to which she responded, 'I have never hoovered anything in my life.' She was the adored baby of the family who had been indulged in everything. Meanwhile, my grandmother hated being stuck in the countryside, with nothing much to do. They just couldn't get used to it.

My mother stayed at Newland Hall while my grandmother and aunt went back to London. My grandmother opened a restaurant in her flat, serving lunch to refugees. That's how they survived. She was a terrific cook. Her parents had run a restaurant in Vienna but it was closed down because anarchists used to go there. Someone was shot and the police closed it down. That was the end of that.

Then my aunt got a job selling stationery – I assume it was with a Jewish firm – which is how she met her husband. She had an appointment at his furniture factory and he fell instantly in love. They got married in 1940.

Later that year, my mother decided she wanted to be in London too. She initially lived with my aunt and her husband in Cedra Court, a 1930s block on Cazenove Road. The Kray twins both had flats there in the 1960s.

My mother found a job working for Anna Freud at the Hampstead War Nurseries she had set up for children affected by the bombings. But then she became pregnant with me.

I arrived in the late autumn of 1941. I was born at Brocket Hall, the stately home turned maternity hospital that had once hosted Von Ribbentrop, Hitler's Minister of Foreign Affairs. I had no idea I was a Brocket Baby until I was an adult, around 50.

Apparently, unmarried mothers were taken from London to Brocket Hall in a charabanc with wooden seats, which must have made for an uncomfortable ride, but my mother was lucky. My uncle drove her there. I was a breech birth. It couldn't have been easy. The wider family were very supportive but nobody visited any of the single women at Brocket Hall.

I recently found a letter from my mother's friend from Austria, Lilly Getzl, who also worked at Newland Hall, written before I was born, in which she talks supportively about my mother's decision to keep me, given my father wasn't on the scene. Many babies born to single mothers were given up for adoption during the war. Perhaps my mother's status – she was still technically married to Richard Krochmalnik – made her feel better able to withstand the stigma.

When Mum and I were allowed to go home, my uncle picked us up and my mother and I went back to the flat in London. My very first memory is of being at the flat during an air raid.

As the war went on, my uncle, who was a wealthy man, decided we would be safer outside London, so he bought a farm in Smallfield near Horley in Surrey. My mother and I joined my aunt and cousin there. My cousin Avril and I were born just seven months apart and we grew up as close as sisters. During the week, my uncle would be working in London but at the weekends he would come and join us.

It was an idyllic sort of childhood. Absolutely privileged. I appreciate now just how privileged it was. I didn't at the time, of course. I remember we had a horse called Sheila, and a black and yellow trap for her to pull along. We had great toys.

The farmland itself was rented to a farmer but we had a large vegetable garden, where we grew lots of food. Avril and I had free rein of the farm. We would wander around and come back indoors when we were hungry. Nobody worried about us. It was a happy time.

I have an early memory of sitting on a tricycle in the garden, between my aunt and uncle, who seemed enormously tall. It was a very grey day and we were watching planes flying past. Since we weren't in the shelter, I think they must have been Allied bombers.

Our farm was on a lane, at the end of which there was a hospital for Canadian soldiers. It was run by the No 14 Canadian General Hospital, a medical unit which, pre-war, had been based in Montreal. Later it was taken over by the No 24 CGH. The Jewish soldiers who were working or being treated there always found their way to us. Or maybe my aunt and mother went to the hospital to find them. We welcomed a house full every Friday night for Shabbat dinner. The soldiers would arrive with gifts from their NAAFI – butter and chocolate. All sorts of things.

I remember one seder night in particular. Seder is the night before Passover, when we eat a special meal and we recite the story of the Jewish people's flight from Egypt. I had a children's book about it and I sat on a soldier's knee and had him read it to me. It's very moving to me to think that many of our Canadian visitors must have gone on to take part in the D-Day landings. There were more than 10,000 Jewish soldiers in the Canadian Army.

Around half a million Jewish men and women served in the US Armed Forces during the war. Arthur, my mother's first cousin, who was a poet by profession, came over from America as a GI. When he had leave, he came to find us in the countryside. He was back in England at the end of the war and on VE Day, he took me and my cousin Avril to see the victory parade in Horley. There were flags flying everywhere. It was such a joyful time but my most vivid memory of the day is that Arthur gave us sticks of cinnamon chewing gum. I never forgot it. I always wished we could get it in England. It took years before it was available here.

With the war over, my aunt and uncle moved back to London, where they'd bought a flat on Baker Street. My mother and I stayed on at the farm. We eventually moved back to London in 1946 but then we all got whooping cough and had to go to Margate to recuperate. That's when my mother met my stepfather, Sydney Newton, who was on holiday in the town. When they married, we moved to Abbey Road. In the 1950s, he built a house in Wembley Park, which he and my mother named Newlands, after Newland Hall.

They couldn't have children but my stepfather – whom I called my father – wanted to have a son. Eventually, they adopted my brother, but I wasn't terribly interested. I was a teenager by then and busy with my own life. The 1950s was the best time. The music was great, as were the clothes, and we all loved dancing.

While I was growing up my mother always spoke to me in English, never in German, but when she was with my grandmother and my aunt and their Viennese friends, she would naturally speak German with them. I picked up some German just by listening in – the Viennese accent is very familiar to me – then I had formal German lessons at school.

I went to Austria for the first time in the late 1940s, when I was around seven or eight. My mother took me to the Alps. She never really wanted to talk about the war and how it had affected Vienna but she did sometimes tell me about the pre-war period and how she and her friends would go ski-ing in the woods outside the city. She was sporty. She always described herself as a 'Wald und Weisen Madchen' – a forest and meadow girl.

For that first trip to Vienna, we travelled by boat and then train, because my mother wouldn't fly. The second time – in 1949 – we went to meet up with her childhood friend Mela, who had spent the war in America, and Mela's new husband. We met them on the train. I remember the tears. It was a very emotional reunion. They were so glad to be together again.

We went to Vienna often when I was older. We spent many long weekends there. My mother was always more relaxed in Austria than in England. She felt she was at home. However she didn't ever take me to the street she had lived on. Perhaps she thought it would be too hard to be in the place where she had last seen her father. My aunt did go there and actually knocked on the door of the old family home. The woman who answered nearly fainted when she saw my aunt. She was a former neighbour, who had always wanted our family's apartment. She protested, 'It wasn't me. I didn't want to live here. *They* said I had to.'

It wasn't until a very long time after the war that we discovered what had happened to my grandfather. We learned that he'd travelled from relative to relative throughout the war and eventually ended up in Budapest. Close to the end of the war he was caught in a round-up and told to get into a truck. He wouldn't. I think he'd just had enough by then. A German guard shot him dead on the spot. His friend, who was with him that day, was taken to a camp but he survived and after the war he wrote to the Red Cross to tell them what had happened. It took them years to trace my mother and pass the news on.

I remember it well, the day she got the letter. I was a teenager then, about 15. My mother was devastated because she had been very close to her father. I think through all those years she'd had a secret hope that he was still alive. My mother's view was that until you know for sure a person's dead, you've got to hope that somehow they're still out there. My grandmother didn't have that hope. She'd always thought her husband was dead.

I knew about the Holocaust at a relatively early age because it wasn't long after the war that survivors starting arriving in England and some of them visited my family. My mother had a cousin called Gustav, who had been in a camp. He came to live in Maida Vale. I heard him talking about it. Other old friends reappeared too. It was from these people that I gradually learned what had happened.

One friend of the family told me how she had been rounded up and sent to Auschwitz with her mother, sister and brother. Mengele, the 'Angel of Death', who performed so many vile experiments on Jewish prisoners, was there when they arrived. He walked up and down the lines making his selections. He asked our friend what she did. She had a flash of inspiration and told him, 'I'm a nurse.' As a result, she was sent to Ravensbruck. The rest of the family was gassed.

People who could work often survived the camps. Mothers with small children were got rid of but those who were strong and healthy and could work were useful.

Over the years I noticed that my mother always avoided watching anything about the war on television. I think she had survivor's guilt. It affected her more and more as the years went by. Anniversaries would trigger her sadness. She spent a lot of time in bed and had to have cognitive therapy in her 70s. It definitely got worse as she got older.

You can feel grief many years after losing a loved one; sometimes even more strongly than you felt it at the time they died. I think that was the case for my mother, with her grief for her father – my grandfather – and all the other friends and family she lost in the Holocaust.

My mother's personality was kind and generous. She and I had a very strong bond because we went through the war together, at a time when she had so recently said 'goodbye' to everything she knew. She said it was a great comfort to have a daughter.

It's important to me for my children to know about our family's history in Vienna. They've been to see the street my mother lived on. The building itself is long gone now, demolished, and replaced by a new block of flats. But it's vital to keep the memory alive. In some way, though hostilities ended long ago, the war is still impacting on our lives.

18

SALVAGE AND SAVINGS

'A cog in the wheel...'

FIGHTING GERMANY WAS EXPENSIVE AND everybody was expected to do their best to help share the cost. That included Britain's children.

A large part of children's contribution to the war effort involved saving resources. At school, paper and pencils were in short supply. They had to be used judiciously. At home, newspapers could not just be thrown away. Once they'd been read, they were cut up into small sheets to be used as toilet paper. This was often a job for a child.

In 1942, the Women's Voluntary Service in London launched a salvage scheme in which schoolchildren were encouraged to collect paper, card and metal. Children who worked especially hard for the scheme were awarded the status of Junior Salvage Steward, which came with a red plastic badge with a cog in the centre embossed with the motto: 'A Cog In The Wheel'. The Cogs, as they became known, even had their own song. To the tune of 'There'll Always Be An England', they sang 'There'll always be a dustbin.'

Around the same time, *Children's Hour* also ran a salvage competition, along the lines of the Blue Peter appeals of more recent years, in which children were asked to collect scrap metal. The winning team collected an impressive nine tonnes of the stuff. It was a brilliant effort, though after the war the news leaked that all those pots and pans Britain's children had requisitioned from their families' kitchens remained unused, joining miles and miles of railings cut down at the start of the war, because they were the wrong sort of metal.

Saving money was important too. Britain's children were encouraged to put their money away via interesting and creative schemes.

During the First World War the National War Savings Committee was established in England and Wales (Scotland and Ireland had their own organisations) to raise money for the war effort in the form of bonds. The committee introduced 'war savings certificates', which were issued by the Post Office and the Trustee Savings Banks. It also oversaw the setting up of local savings associations, run by volunteers. Between 1914 and 1918, over £400 million was saved.

At the end of the First World War, the certificates were rebranded as 'National Savings Certificates' and the income they raised was redirected into national infrastructure projects.

Upon the outbreak of World War Two, a new 'War Savings' campaign was quickly introduced and volunteers were recruited to administer the scheme at a local level. Savings stamps could be bought for as little as sixpence. Fifteen shillings' worth could be exchanged for a National Savings Certificate. If you collected as much as £5 worth of stamps, you would be issued with a 'Defence Bond'. The idea was that your savings were guaranteed to give you a good return when the war was over.

To encourage people to invest, the savings groups held special themed weeks. For example, there was a 'Warship Week' and a 'Wings For Victory' week. Savings targets were then set to fund specific pieces of military equipment, such as a particular plane. In Spitfire Week, national savers were set a target of £5,000, the cost of a new Spitfire. If they had saved enough, local groups could 'adopt' ships and planes.

War baby Ann Hay recalls her own response to Spitfire Week, 'A special five-shilling coin was issued, the Churchill crown. I decided I wanted to send mine to Mr Churchill himself to buy him a Spitfire. My mother said she'd turn my crown piece into a postal order and we sent the postal order and my letter to Mr Churchill. I got a letter of thanks from his Private Secretary. Years later, I found my mother hadn't actually parted with the Churchill crown but had used my sixpence a week pocket money instead. I was convinced I'd paid for a whole Spitfire (they cost £5,000) but remember I was five. There is a Mark 1 Spitfire at an airfield near Maidenhead, and I reckon that's mine – well, maybe a couple of rivets!'

In Chorlton-cum-Hardy, Vera Hogg and her brother Alan also threw themselves into the war effort, as Vera explained in a letter written many years later.

'At the start of the war, Alan and I were evacuated. I can remember my mother writing our names on our clothes and gas masks and kit bags with which we were issued. We assembled at our school and were taken by bus to Derbyshire. There we had to wait until we were allocated accommodation with the local people. My brother and I were at different homes as the people concerned could only accommodate two girls or two boys but we were only about two houses away. We were well looked after and it was a new experience to be in the countryside. Our parents were able to visit about once a fortnight. We kept in touch with our new friends for many years.

As things seemed to have quietened down (not so many air raids) our parents decided to have us home for Christmas but unfortunately that was the time of the Manchester Blitz which was quite frightening for two young children. We would be awakened by the sirens and would quickly get dressed in warm clothes which were kept ready and then down into the air raid shelter.

After this we were evacuated again to a place called Edgeworth near Bolton and once more we were fortunate in getting good homes with kind people, although again we were separated but not far apart. Where I stayed the people kept a few animals. They had two calves, one of which they allowed me to call my own; some hens and chickens, a goat, ferrets and a dog. This again was a new experience for me.

In front of the house was a steep field and during the winter we were able to sledge here. The lady I was staying with became ill so again I had to be moved where I wasn't too happy, so our parents brought me and Alan home, where we stayed.'

Back in Chorlton cum Hardy, Vera and Alan helped in the gathering of salvage and collected for the Blind Children Society. Aged only 13, Alan became secretary of the 'Grindley Avenue No 2 Savings Group'. To encourage their friends and neighbours to save, Alan made his own posters and leaflets in which he extolled the virtue of saving in wartime in poetry. One of those poems, written in collaboration with Vera, was entitled 'Wings for Victory':

> *Wings for victory week is near,*
> *Buy your savings stamps from here,*
> *And your husbands, sons and daughters,*
> *Will get Hitler at close quarters,*
> *Manchester's aim £11,000,000 pounds*
> *Will buy more planes to bomb Hitler's grounds.*
> *So save your money,*
> *And do not worry,*
> *Those wings we need in a terrible hurry.*

By the time Alan and Vera wrote that poem, they had already raised far more than their initial £20 target. Alan's leaflet proudly states, 'Total savings from September 20th 1942 to February 28th 1943 = £121 11s 6d.

Alan's enthusiasm was unstoppable and soon the Grindley Avenue savings group was awarded a 'Certification of Honour' signed by Archibald Sinclair, the Secretary of State for Air, marking the collection of £435 (roughly equivalent to £25,350 in today's money). Who knows what Alan might have gone on to achieve.

Vera wrote, 'Alan was tragically killed in a road accident at the age of 13.' He was knocked down and killed by a bus, while out delivering papers on his bicycle.

His obituary in the local paper – the City News – was entitled 'A Great Little Fellow'. A senior member of the Savings Club described Alan thus, 'one of the gayest, most efficient, hard-working little chaps I have had the pleasure of knowing.'

19

THE BETHNAL GREEN DISASTER

'Stairway to Heaven...'

DURING THE BLITZ, THE MANY tens of thousands of Anderson and Morrison shelters which had been distributed up and
down the country were put to good use, but in the big cities, where
many people lived in small flats or houses without gardens, public
shelters were very important. But where to put them? In London,
the underground offered the ready-made solution. The platforms
made perfect shelters. In 1939, the Central Line was still under
construction, but many of its stations were almost finished. These
included Bethnal Green station in East London.

When the local council was considering its shelter provision,
it was initially decided that Bethnal Green station did not reach
proper safety standards. The brand-new station had only one
entrance, with two more yet to be built. However, when the Blitz
began, there was no time to make the necessary adjustments and it
was decided that the station should be used after all, as it was, with
police officers manning the entrance to make sure that when the
sirens sounded people entered in an orderly manner.

Soon thousands of people were using Bethnal Green during air raids. The station could accommodate 10,000, with triple-decker bunk beds for 5,000 on the platforms and in the as-yet unused tube tunnels. As the Blitz went on, all manner of facilities were added to the shelter to improve the experience of those who had to sleep there. It had a first aid post and a doctor's surgery, a canteen, a library and even a small theatre, which put on shows to distract residents from the horror going on at ground level.

By 1943, in the lull between the Blitz and the arrival of the V1s, the number of people who slept in the Bethnal Green shelter overnight had dwindled to a few hundred and, due to the pressures of conscription which meant that more and more young men and women were being called up, there was no longer a permanent police presence at the shelter entrance. There didn't seem to be a need.

At the beginning of March 1943, the Allies had bombed Berlin and Britain expected some sort of revenge, just as Hitler had exacted on Coventry after the bombing of Munich. With this in mind, while they might previously have waited the raids out at home, many more people than usual headed for the Bethnal Green Shelter when the siren sounded just after 8pm on March 3rd.

As the crowds were filing down the steps, three full buses arrived and their passengers poured out, hopeful of finding shelter underground. Just as that was happening, anti-aircraft rockets were fired from Victoria Park and the unexpected sound, which many people assumed was from enemy fire, sent people scrambling for the poorly lit staircase down into the station.

At the bottom of the staircase, a woman with a child stumbled and fell, pulling an elderly man down with her. Within seconds other people were falling on top of them. Crushed by the weight of those who came after them and unable to draw breath, people began to fall into unconsciousness.

The people already safely installed on the platforms knew nothing about the nightmare unfolding on the stairs. Wardens tried to pull survivors out of the crush from the bottom. Police officers tried from the top. It was too late. The final death toll was 173, of whom 62 were children, toddlers and babies. The youngest victim was Carol Geary, a babe in arms, just five months old.

The disaster at Bethnal Green was the deadliest incident involving civilians in the whole war. In the days that followed, the government, fearing for the effect on public morale (and the exposure of alleged Government failings), was able to keep the news of the disaster from being very widely known. It's only recently that a memorial to the victims, called the Stairway To Heaven, has been erected at the site. But for the people of Bethnal Green, particularly children such as Doreen Middleton, the scars of the disaster still remain.

Doreen Middleton, 92

I GREW UP IN BETHNAL Green. At the beginning of the war, my family was living in a flat opposite Victoria Park.

Because it was so near to London's docklands and the City it was obvious that Bethnal Green might be a target for the German bombers, so the children from my school were ready to be evacuated weeks before war was declared. We went to school every day with our suitcases and our labels. When the moment came, we gathered in the playground and marched to the railway station. Our parents didn't know where we were going to be sent. Mum came to see us off but Dad was at work. I found out years later that when he heard which station we were being sent from, he raced over there to say 'goodbye' to me, only to see the train pulling out.

When we arrived at our destination, somewhere near Oxford, we waited in the playground to be matched with our foster families. Each family was supposed to take two children so sibling pairs went first. I had a brother but he was back in London with Mum because he was only a baby, born in January 1939. That meant I was on my own and because of that, I was one of the last to be picked. I was only six and thought I was going to have to stay in the playground all night in the dark.

Eventually a woman did take me home, along with another evacuee – a little boy. I had very thick long brown hair in those days and when the woman got us back to her house, she went at it with a nit comb. I had to do my best not to cry. She thought people from London were dirty. It's ironic really because her house didn't even have piped water. They had one outside pump for four cottages.

I'd been enjoying school in London but we were told by the village school that they didn't have room for us London kids. It wouldn't have been too bad since I'd already learned to read but there were no books in the house I was staying in. They didn't even have a daily paper. We were left to play all day and I was bullied quite badly by the little boy I had to share with. I was very unhappy.

One day we had a raid and I woke up to all this noise and banging and I was terrified – too terrified to move – I could see the search lights on the ceiling and hear the guns and eventually someone came up to get me and said, 'Oh, we left you because you were asleep.'

Back in London at around the same time, our flat near Victoria Park was bombed out. While the building was empty looters got in and took Mum's watch and five shillings of savings. It was a lot to lose because we didn't have much. The looters even took the cutlery.

Even though all this was going on, when Dad came to visit me in Oxford and saw how unhappy I was, he decided he would take me home. By then the family had moved to a house next to a sawmill. I think that's why I always had bronchitis and asthma growing up.

On my first night back in London, there was an air-raid warning. Dad woke me up and carried me over to the shelter. After that, I learned to leave my coat and my shoes ready, so I could put them on and dash over.

Dad had been turned down for the army because of bad health but that didn't mean he didn't do war work. He worked at the Old Ford sawmill during the day and by night he had to be on fire watch there too. We hardly ever saw him.

On one occasion when Dad was home and did come over to the shelter with us, the all clear went and we emerged to a dark red sky. I asked Dad why the sky looked so strange and he said, 'It's all the fires.' That was the night they'd tried to bomb St Paul's, which was only half a mile away.

Another night, Mum woke me up and said, 'the siren's been,' but I didn't get up quickly enough. We could already hear the shrapnel falling. We couldn't risk going outside then so Mum grabbed my baby brother and we sat on the stairs all night. I don't know what good that would have done, sitting on the stairs. We couldn't sit under the stairs because the cupboard was full of coal.

At least we had coal that time. Once Mum was out queuing for food when the coalman came. If you weren't in you didn't get any coal for another month and it was freezing cold. Dad ended up looking round for anything to burn. Going up to my bedroom was like going into a fridge. Dad bought me a hot water bottle. Not a rubber one but stone. It was alright while it was warm but when it went cold and you knocked your foot against it, it used to hurt. When it went round that they were digging up the asphalt on a road where we children used to roller-skate, we rushed round with prams and things and took tar blocks to put on the fire.

When the raids were at their height, we'd go over to the shelter every night. Then we found out that you could sleep down in the Tube, which seemed a safer option. Our nearest Tube station was the newly built Bethnal Green on the Central Line. The Central Line hadn't yet got that far east so there were no tracks in the tunnel, which made it easy to set up sleeping quarters for thousands of people there. I do remember that it was a really deep station – or so it seemed to me as a child. There was a huge escalator but it wasn't operational so you had to walk down it like it was stairs. I hated going down it. It seemed such a long way down.

We were allocated bunk beds and spent many nights down there. It wasn't very comfortable but Mum felt safer deep underground than in the shelter on our road. She must have thought our family had had enough near misses after getting bombed out of the flat.

At the end of February 1943, I caught a cold that wouldn't seem to shift. It can't have helped spending night after night in the tube tunnel, crammed in with all those other people. It was easy for colds and flu to spread. On March 3rd 1943, I still wasn't better so Mum told Dad, 'I'm not taking Doreen down the shelter tonight. It's very damp down there.'

That cold I had saved our lives because that was the night the disaster happened. Apparently they were trying out a new type of gun in Victoria Park and it made such a peculiar noise, people thought it must be a new enemy weapon. They rushed to get into the station in a panic. There were no handrails on the stairs and a woman fell down with her baby. Dozens of people tumbled down after her and 173 were suffocated in the resulting crush. My uncle Ernie was in the local ARP and he had to go and deal with the bodies.

The disaster wasn't in the papers or on the radio news because Churchill suppressed it for the sake of national morale but of course we knew all about it because my uncle had been there with the ARP. And everyone spoke to their neighbours in those days so the news spread like wildfire. People were very angry. I heard my aunts and Mum talking about it. We didn't go into a tube shelter again.

After that, I was evacuated once more. This time I went with Mum and my baby brother near Leake in Staffordshire. The couple we lodged with resented Londoners. Mum, my brother and I were all squashed into one room. Mum wasn't allowed to use the kitchen so we had to cook over the fire in our bedroom.

Every day we'd walk the five or six miles into Leake; Mum pushing my brother in his pram. Once we met some fellow Londoners on a dark country lane and stopped for a chat. When we got back to the house at nine, the couple had locked us out in the cold. We had to pummel on the door!

The following morning, there was heavy snow and Mum had to get a shovel to dig a path to the outside loo. That was the final straw. When Dad came down to visit, Mum told him, 'I'm coming home.'

I remember that on the way home, we had to change trains at Crewe. My brother had been sick all over me. We were very tired and you never knew when a train was going to come. As we waited for our connection, a soldier put his coat over me to keep me warm. That was the thing about the war: we experienced both horrible meanness and great generosity.

In 1944, we were back in the shelter on our street and it was taking a very long time for the all-clear to sound, even though it didn't sound as though there were bombers overheard. Eventually, we heard on the grapevine that a plane had crashed just down Roman Road, which wasn't far from us, but they couldn't find the pilot. That was the first doodlebug.

When the doodlebugs were coming over, you'd get the air raid siren and then the local claxon if it was coming your way. You'd hear the drone of the doodlebug's engine and then it would stop and your heart would stop with it. You counted to 10 and then you heard the bang and you knew you were still alive. We just accepted it as kids. If we heard the drone of doodlebugs, we'd grab our dinner and run over to the shelter on our road.

I failed my 11 plus so when I was old enough I went to Daniel Street School. Though it was a mixed school, boys and girls were separated. The boys had the bottom half of the building and we girls had the top half. The girls' playground was on the roof.

Shortly after I started at Daniel Street, the V2s began to come over. They'd land at any time of the day or night. I remember we were having a cookery lesson when a rocket landed nearby. The shock sent all our rolling pins rolling onto the floor.

The infamous Kray twins - Ronnie and Reggie - were pupils at Daniel Street too. They were in the same year as me and I'd talk to them from time to time. They were just ordinary kids back then. Everybody knew them because they were identical twins but there was no sign of the gangsters they'd become.

Years later, when one of the Kray twins died, my brother and I saw some footage of his funeral on the television. My brother turned and asked me, 'Was that the church opposite the Bethnal Green library?' I told him it was. It was the church where Mum and Dad got married. My brother then told me that he used to go into that church to wash his hands in the font before going to borrow a book, because we had to show our hands were clean before we were allowed to take books out.

The year 1944 was a year of close shaves for our family.

One weekend, I was at home and Mum heard on the one o'clock news that a rocket had gone off down Roman Road, which was where our uncle Cyril lived. Mum wanted to check he was alright so we headed straight down there. Although I'd been used to playing on bomb sites, among all the rubble and shrapnel, where you'd see half a house and someone's bedroom wallpaper, I was horrified by what we saw that afternoon. This rocket had taken out the whole street. Instead of just three or four houses the whole street had gone. I remember it had a big impact on me. The sheer destruction.

Shortly after that, Mum was at her temp job at Woolworths at Aldwych when we heard on the news that a rocket had fallen in Aldwych. We went tearing up there. Thankfully, the rocket hit the corner opposite Woollies that day and Mum was unscathed.

Then the pub opposite my aunt's house got a direct hit and she and Dad, who was visiting, had to be dug out of the cellar. Yes, we had numerous near misses but everyone got through the war.

Towards the end of the war, I used to go and do errands for mum before school. On this particular morning, I can remember vividly Mum saying, 'Don't be long because there's going to be an important announcement.' When I got back, I saw that she'd torn two pics of Montgomery out of a newspaper and stuck them on the wall. Then we heard the announcement that the war was over. All the neighbours came out to talk about it.

On May 8th, we celebrated in style. Someone dragged a piano out into the street. The women rustled up sandwiches. There was singing and dancing. As it got dark, some of the men lit a big bonfire and we went on singing around that until the fire brigade came and put our fire out. We'd been through the bombs, the doodlebugs and the rockets but they said our fire was too dangerous!

At some point in the early evening, I told Mum I was tired. She suggested I have a lay down and come back out to carry on celebrating later. But when I woke up it was the following day. It was my birthday and I was 12. There was no money for presents and now that VE Day was behind us, everyone had gone back to work.

A few days later, Mum, Dad, my brother and I went to see the lights turned back on at Piccadilly Circus. There was still wreckage everywhere. I remember walking down Barnet Road shortly after VE Day. It was so dark and grey. Then I came to the oil shop, which sold oil for lamps and candles. That sort of thing. They must have just had a delivery of washing up bowls. They were piled up outside the shop and they were such a lovely cherry red that I stopped to stare at them. Life was so dreary post-war that if you went to the cinema and a film in colour was playing, it was jubilation!

The war in Europe was over but life didn't quite go back to normal for me for a while. I saw the school doctor and he said I was undernourished so I was sent off to convalesce in Haslemere for three months. I was there over VJ Day. No-one was allowed to visit me. I had to put on five pounds in weight before I was allowed back home.

When I think about how the war affected me personally, I feel lucky in that no-one in my immediate family was killed but I'm very upset about my lack of education. Because of all the bombing there wasn't really much schooling going on.

As you got towards the end of school, you saw a careers teacher but they didn't offer you much choice: it was dressmaking and machining for girls and bricklaying for boys. I came top of my class but no-one gave me the opportunity to go on to further education. In my last school report, the headmistress wrote, 'Doreen should do well at the work she's chosen,' but I didn't get to choose what I did! I didn't even get to stay on until I turned 16, as my brother would. No-one cared about the girls. Especially not girls like me.

It was political, in my view. There was this idea that the people of the East End could do all the odd jobs, the hard jobs. My parents' generation accepted their fate because they didn't have the education that you have to ask for things. They used to look up to what we called the 'white collar' workers but the white collar workers didn't have their best interests at heart. My dad went in one day soon after the war, after fire-watching for all those years and never having a day off, and got the sack. He went in, they said 'we're restructuring' and he was just given his cards. No redundancy money or anything. All that effort. He got nothing in return. I feel quite bitter about that.

I left school on a Friday and started working in a dress-making factory on the Monday. The women who worked in that factory were on piece-work, where workers are paid per unit produced. I didn't last long there. I struggled to get the hang of what I was supposed to be doing and was given the sack for being too slow.

I got a good hiding for the disgrace of losing my job. In retrospect, that turned out to be a blessing in disguise, because I went on to work at the Baltic Shipping Exchange in the City. I started out running errands around the office but soon learned to take calls on the switchboard and how to type. I went to evening classes, which is where I met my husband. When we talked about the war, we discovered that while I was sleeping at Bethnal Green on the central line, my husband was sleeping at Liverpool Street, one stop up.

As I got older, I started to think more critically about the way Britain was. It was clear that if you had money you could get whatever you wanted. My dad worked hard but he never had a car, never owned his own house, in spite of all his work. It was terrible, the way he was treated.

Even the war itself was different for the rich. One thing that really upset me was knowing how hard it was for my mum to get enough food for my baby brother during the war. He was always hungry. Yet if you had money, you could go to a restaurant and buy a meal. I thought that was totally unfair.

Even when I had a good job, my lack of formal education continued to haunt me. When I was in my fifties and my daughters were teenagers, taking their O levels, I got really interested in what they were learning. I joined an evening class on 'reading for pleasure', with an excellent teacher who introduced me to lots of new books and plays. I got a thirst for theatre. Poetry too. I remember listening to Richard Burton reading *Under Milk Wood*. That was magical. I read *Jude the Obscure* by Thomas Hardy too. That was ironic, remembering my own experience of Oxford and its dreaming spires. I certainly didn't get an education there.

As the course went on, the teacher saw how much I enjoyed reading and encouraged me to take an O level in English literature. I was working evenings then. I would get home at midnight and stay up writing my essays for the next day. I passed my exams. But I still resent that I didn't get an education and the government didn't make it up to us kids after the war. I always resented that. So many of us missed out on so much.

I do think what my generation experienced still isn't fully appreciated. My daughter works as a tour guide in London. She had some American clients who told her, 'We won't forget what your mum's generation went through. Tell her we won't forget.' That meant a lot to me.

20

BRITAIN'S SCHOOLS UNDER FIRE

'Plucked before the petals fall...'

THERE'S NO DOUBT THAT EDUCATION was a casualty of war. Many thousands of school buildings were requisitioned for war purposes, for use by the military or to hold civilians bombed out of their homes. It's estimated that one in five schools in Britain was damaged by bombing too. The list of schools where lives were lost is shockingly long.

It's only recently that the details of a bombing raid on South Hallsville School in Canning Town have been made public, having been kept secret to maintain morale and deprive Hitler of a useful piece of propaganda. On the night of September 10th 1940, hundreds of children and adults were gathered at the school ahead of a new evacuation. The school had a large basement that was used as a public shelter. A German fighter plane dropped a parachute bomb on the school that caused the building to collapse. Officially, 77 people lost their lives. However, a great many of the dead were not retrieved from the wreckage and rumours started circulating that the number of casualties was much higher. The crater left by the bomb was filled in. Today, it's believed that as many as 600 people may have died at South Hallsville School, making it the largest civilian disaster of the war.

In October that same year, seven children lost their lives when Alfred Street Junior School in Rushden, Northampton, was hit by a stray bomb. Three of those children were evacuees from Colchester.

A month later, Liverpool was in the Luftwaffe's sights. On the night of November 29th 1940, the important port city faced eight solid hours of bombing. Around 300 people had taken shelter in the basement of the Ernest Brown Junior Instructional College in Durning Road, which took a direct hit by a parachute mine that was possibly meant for a nearby railway station. The three-storey building crumbled and escape and rescue attempts were hampered further when the college's furnaces exploded, spewing scalding water – 166 people were killed.

In March of 1941, Bankhead Primary School in Knightswood, an area of Glasgow, Scotland, was one of the first buildings to be hit during what became known as the Clydebank Blitz, possibly because of its proximity to a railway depot. Over March 13th and 14th, Clydebank was targeted by 400 Luftwaffe bombers. Thousands were made homeless and 528 were killed. Bankhead Primary School was, thankfully, not being used as a school at the time of the attack – it had been requisitioned for a civil defence station – but the 39 people who were killed there included a five-year-old and two boy messengers, Ronaldo Pacitti and Daniel Woodhead, who had been assisting the ARP.

On September 29th 1942, 32 people, including 28 boys, were killed when a Junkers 88 dropped its bombs on Petworth Boys School West Sussex. It's believed the bomber's actual target was a top secret meeting at nearby Petworth House.

And on January 20th 1943, Sandhurst Road School in Catford was targeted by a German bomber, which dropped a 1,100lb bomb on the school at lunchtime. Thirty-two children died at the school and six more died later in hospital. Six staff were also killed.

The attack on Sandhurst Road School was believed to be a German '*Terrorangriff*' – an opportunistic attack intended to cause maximum disruption and fear. The German pilot who attacked the school, Hauptmann Heinz Schumann, claimed to have targeted the school thinking it might be a factory but eyewitnesses reported that a German plane strafed the playground before the bomb was dropped on the part of the school where many children were eating their lunch. Reporting on the tragedy, The Kentish Mercury headline described the loss of the children thus: 'Plucked before the petals fall.'

With schools under fire in the cities and under strain in the countryside, the Government became increasingly concerned that Britain's children were falling behind and it was decided that something had to be done to prevent a serious overall drop in the population's literacy and numeracy, particularly among children from poorer families.

A new plan for post-war secondary education in Britain was pushed through Parliament by Education Minister RA Butler. The Education Act of 1944, which was followed by a similar Act for Scotland, provided for free secondary education for all, regardless of socioeconomic background. Most importantly, it increased the school-leaving age to 15 years old, so that no child would have to go to work in a factory at 14, as Doreen Middleton had to.

The Education Act was not perfect and certainly would not bring true equality. Pupils were still to be streamed by the 11 plus and grammar school pupils would continue to have an advantage when it came to choosing a path through life, but the raising of the school leaving age would at least benefit pupils like Doreen's friend, evacuee Norma Nunn.

Norma Nunn, 95

IN 1939, WE WERE LIVING with my maternal grandmother – Nan – on Bothwell Street near the Fulham Palace Road in London. My father William was a striking man, an only child and quite spoiled by his parents, and he was always being unfaithful. He and my mum Alice were forever separating and getting back together, which meant we were always having to move. Before I was school-age, I'd lived in five different houses. After move number five, I stayed with Nan.

While Dad didn't have any brothers and sisters, my mum came from a big family. She had six brothers and one sister (another sister had died) and there were 18 children in my generation. I was born in 1930, the eldest of five siblings. My brother William, who we called Joe, was a year younger and John Edward arrived three years after him. Our little sister Yvonne was born right before the war. Our youngest brother, Keith, was born after the war was over.

Mum's was a close family. My aunt and all my uncles lived near Nan and they were always in and out of each other's houses. We had a tradition where everyone would gather at Nan's on a Saturday night for a bit of a party. Nan had a piano. We all knew how to play and there was always someone banging out a tune so we could sing along.

I remember the run-up to the war quite clearly. Several shelters were built on our road. During the school holidays, I'd played in them with my friends. I'd also heard the possibility of war being talked about at home, when my aunts and uncles came round. Nan and the other grown-ups didn't try to hide anything from me and I do remember being worried about what was going on. Mum must have been worried too because she decided we should be evacuated as soon as we could. I left London with Mum, my two brothers and my baby sister on September 1st, two days before war was declared. Mum was able to come with us because Yvonne was still so small.

I can still remember the day we left, how busy the station was with people trying to get out of London, all the children carrying little cases and everyone with their gas masks around their necks. Some of the smaller children had Mickey Mouse masks.

We were taken by bus to a village near Brackley in Northampton-shire called Syresham, where the local people were waiting to greet us. If you had a spare room, you were expected to take an evacuee or two in, whether you wanted to or not. Mum, my siblings and I were billeted in 'The Gate House', which was owned by a Mrs Corey, whose husband was a captain in the army. The servants who usually lived in the Gate House had been called up, so we stayed in their quarters.

We had two bedrooms between the five of us. Mum, my sister and I shared one bedroom and the boys had the other. Down-stairs we had a kitchen and a living room with orange carpet and curtains. I loved it straightaway. I felt quite safe there, though until that day I'd never really been outside London, except to Bushy Park or Brighton for the day, and to spend a week in Norfolk with a relative who worked in a hotel.

I loved being in the countryside. Syresham was surrounded by fields filled with cows. I loved the freedom we had there. You could roam all over the place to play and not come home until it was dark. You didn't have to worry about anything.

My brothers and I joined the local school, which had doubled in size with us new arrivals, so that some classes had to be held in the Chapel Sunday School. The headmaster, a Welshman called Mr Williams, was kind but strict. The teachers were all very friend-ly but the local children were a bit wary of us at first. They'd had very different lives to us Londoners. The poorer children didn't have much time to play because they were expected to work on their family farms after school and at the weekends. Children from better off families didn't go to the village school but were sent to nearby Brackley.

Everyone made an effort to bring the evacuees and the local children together. We went to Sunday School, with Mr Brody the vicar. The Londoners organised school sports and put on plays. An after-school club, called the Nor-Londer Club, gathered weekly in the church hall. There was a piano in the hall. One of the boys would play one hand of a tune and I would play the other – the left hand usually. I also joined the Red Cross cadets, learning first aid, which I thought might come in useful later on.

One of my closest friends was Betty, another evacuee. She was billeted in a different village – Crowfield – and had to walk over the fields to get home from school at the end of the day. I would often go with her, walking her halfway so that we got to spend as much time together as possible. Because the blackout was in operation, as the days got shorter it got very dark on that walk, with no torches allowed, and on one occasion, Betty fell over a horse that had been sleeping on the ground.

When we arrived in Syresham in September 1939, everyone was expecting that London would be bombed in the next few days or weeks but by Christmas it was all still pretty quiet. We went back to Fulham to be with Nan for the holidays and, since nothing happened while we were there, Mum decided that we should stay on.

Mum and Dad weren't together then and Mum had met a Swiss man called Charlie Lustig, who worked as a waiter on a ship. In 1940, Charlie joined the Merchant Navy. Being Swiss, he didn't have to join the forces. The tragedy is, he died before his first voyage when the boat he was working on was sunk while it was still in the harbour.

Then, in the summer of 1940, the Battle of Britain started and after all those months of nothing much happening, London was suddenly being bombed.

Whenever the air raid siren sounded, we would rush to the shelter in my aunt's back garden, since there was no shelter at the back of the house where we were living with Nan. As soon as we heard the siren, we'd grab what we needed and go. Nan once told me to grab a blanket and I brought out her favourite eiderdown, which was the wrong thing to do because the eiderdown was beautifully white and the shelter was a bit dirty. It was an Anderson shelter, made of corrugated iron, with earth heaped all over the top. They had nothing in them when they were first built. You had to furnish them yourself, so my grandfather had made benches to go along each side for us to sit or even sleep on while we waited the air raids out.

During a raid, the adults chatted and joked and played cards to while away the hours. We were a very jolly family and the party spirit that filled Nan's house on a Saturday night came with us to the shelter. I never felt unsafe so long as Nan was in there with us. Sometimes, the men of the family weren't there though. Granddad worked on the underground so he would often spend the air raids down in the tunnels.

Once I woke up all on my own in the shelter and convinced myself I must have died. There was no other explanation. Everyone else was gone. Vanished. I thought I must be on the other side. Of course, when I went into the house, I found all the grown-ups in the kitchen, laughing and joking and making tea. They'd just decided to let me sleep on rather than wake me up and bring me inside when the all-clear sounded.

Having lost Charlie and with the air raids getting worse, Mum decided we needed to get out of London again. She phoned Mrs Corey and asked if we could have our old billet.

Mum took me back to the Gate House, along with my little sister. My brothers, for some reason, went instead to Wales. Like Mum, Mrs Corey was grieving. Her eldest son had been killed in Crete.

By this time, three of Mum's brothers, my uncles, had been called up. My uncle Jack, who had four children, got a job training soldiers. My uncles Stan and Ernest also joined the army. I was especially close to Uncle Ernest, who was father to Joyce, the eldest of us cousins. I knew Uncle Ernest very well because he was always coming to Nan's house to bring Joyce home whenever she ran away to come and play with me.

Little by little, as the Blitz continued, other members of the family were bombed out of their homes and moved to Syresham too. When my uncles were home on leave, they would come to the country and the whole family would be back together again in the local pub, turning the Kings Head into a corner of London for the night.

Nan came and joined us when her house was condemned. The house itself wasn't hit but a bomb that went off further down the street had left it so unsteady it wasn't safe to live in any more. Nan brought all our furniture with her and it was stored in a barn nearby.

We were much safer from air raids in Syresham than we had been in Fulham, but that didn't mean we didn't see anything of the war. There were several air stations nearby – there was an RAF café in the village and we would often see the RAF planes heading off to tackle the Germans. We also saw American airmen driving through on the way to their base at RAF Podington. There was an Italian POW camp nearby too. The Italian prisoners wore brown uniforms with yellow patches. They would make baskets which they'd sell to the villagers. They were very friendly to us children.

A round of six bombs was dropped close to the viaduct in Helmdon, a village just four miles away. Eventually, Syresham did get its own bomb too, when a Luftwaffe bomber, returning to Germany after a raid, dropped a bomb in the village. They would sometimes do that – off-load bombs they hadn't used at random before flying home. This bomb landed right near the church. It exploded but luckily no-one was hurt and afterwards we children were pleased to have shrapnel to collect.

Despite the rationing, we didn't ever go hungry in Syresham. Though we only got one rasher of bacon and one egg in our rations, there was always milk because we were surrounded by dairy farms. Extra eggs weren't hard to come by either. One of my aunts had a dog that would go off wandering in the village and come back with an egg in its mouth, which it would deposit on the doorstep. I don't know how the dog managed to carry the eggs without ever breaking them. Sometimes we would have a chicken, though I'm not sure we were supposed to. In the autumn, we would collect windfall apples and go scrumping for plums. The hardest thing about rationing for me was not getting as much tea and sweets as I was used to.

When we first arrived in Syresham in 1939, my brother Joe got himself a job looking after the animals on a nearby farm. When I returned to Syresham in 1940, with Joe by then in Wales, I took over his job. At the end of each school day and on Saturday mornings, I would muck out the chickens and the cows and make sure they were all fed. The cows were lovely, Guernsey, fawn in colour with big dark eyes. I loved them. At the end of the week, I'd get four shillings in wages, which I would spend on a trip to the pictures in Towcester, followed by tea and cake in a café. You had to be careful to make sure you didn't miss the bus home because it was a seven mile walk back.

When I was old enough, I took the 11 plus and won a place at a school in Northampton. It was actually a London technical college, based in Paddington, that had been relocated to Northampton for the war. I needed a new uniform to go to this new school, which was awkward because of rationing, but we discovered that the first thing we'd make in needlework lessons was a smock we could use instead. It had every stitch in it and pleats and darts, the idea being that it would be a chance to learn different kinds of sewing.

I couldn't go back and forth from Syresham every day so I had to stay in the city during the week. To begin with, I stayed with a young woman whose husband was away at the war, and her son, who was around six or seven years old. After that, I lodged with a married couple – Mr and Mrs Harris – along with some other girls. The food at their house was pretty terrible. One night every week, Mrs Harris would give us money to go to the fish and chip shop. It was never quite enough but, as we were heading out, her husband would always slip us a little bit of extra money to make up the difference.

Around this time, Mum brought my brothers back from Wales to live in Syresham. We were astonished when they both turned up speaking with Welsh accents, since they hadn't been living there for very long. But my brother Joe was always a very good mimic – he and I used to like to do impressions of people we knew – so that must have helped him pick up the accent up.

I was still at the technical college, going back and forth from Northampton to Syresham at the weekends when VE Day came around. I very much wanted to be back in Syresham in time for the party but something happened that meant I missed my bus and didn't get back until late in the evening. Fortunately, everyone was still celebrating.

Now that the war was over, it was time to go back to London.

I would have liked to stay in the countryside for a bit longer but the technical college was closing down. I had to go to a school in Hammersmith instead. I stayed on until I was 16, then I left to take a job as a dressmaker at Bradleys of Bayswater. I made some good friends and on a Friday night we would go dancing at the Hammersmith Palais. That's where I met my husband.

My husband was about 10 years older than me and he'd served in the armed forces during the war. It wasn't until years after we married that he told me he'd been at the Battle of Monte Cassino. People didn't talk much about what they'd done in the war in those days. I think we all wanted to forget about it and move on to happier times.

Looking back, I can see that those years in Syresham really made their mark on me but in a good way. They gave me my love of the countryside. I've always loved hiking in the great outdoors. I made some good friends too, some of whom I stayed in touch with up until they passed away. I went back to Syresham a few years ago. The Kings Head pub, where my relatives recreated a little bit of London at the weekends, still looks exactly the same.

21

OPERATION BOLERO

'Got any gum, chum?'

BY THE BEGINNING OF 1944, the 100,000 GIs who had arrived in 1942, had been joined by 1.4 million further US troops in a strategic build-up of American forces and equipment in Britain codenamed *Operation Bolero*.

All over Britain, the Americans were now a familiar sight, as the country was turned into a gigantic military base, with new airfields, training facilities, supply depots and hospitals to service the new arrivals being built at an astonishing rate. Britain's roads and lanes were busy with American jeeps. Tonnes of supplies and equipment were moved to the coast in preparation for an Allied invasion of Nazi-occupied Europe.

In East Anglia, where the flatness of the land was perfect for airfields (runways were built using rubble from bombed out London), 400,000 GIs awaited their orders to move into occupied Europe. One person who saw their preparations for D-Day up close was nine-year-old Derek Hull, from Essex.

Derek Hull, 90

AS A YOUNG LAD GROWING up in Brentwood, I thought the war was a bit of an adventure. When it started, I was still at junior school. That's where I had my first experience of going into a shelter during an air raid. It was a proper underground shelter that had been built for the First World War. There were Zeppelin battles over Brentwood in 1916. Anyway, we all trotted down there with our gas masks. You always had to have your gas mask with you, no matter where you were.

Brentwood is only 20 miles from London but at the beginning of the war it was considered to be a safe place to send evacuees. We lived in a two-bedroom terraced house, on Queen's Road near the Spread Eagle pub. It was only just big enough for Mum, me and my older brother and sister, but in September 1939, Mum was told she'd have to give up the front room to an evacuated family from the East End: a mother and her two children.

It didn't go well. The children weren't very friendly and we started to notice a strange musty smell around the house that got worse over the time they were with us. Eventually, Mum realised that the smell was being caused by bed-bugs, which the evacuees had brought with them from London. We all had to move out and the house had to be fumigated with this horrible yellow gas before we could move back in again. I don't know what happened to the evacuees. The Blitz hadn't started then so they might have gone back to London.

Brentwood was an important town in those days because of Warley Barracks, where lots of troops were training, so the powers that be decided it needed to have proper defences. In the summer of 1940, they put up concrete and steel barriers all around the town in a ring so it could be closed off if needed. We had anti-tank emplacements too, which were manned by the Home Guard.

When the Blitz started, the railway from Brentwood into London was a target for the Germans so the area around the station got bombed from the beginning. It got worse in October 1940, when we had bombing most of the month. I remember the sound of the air raid siren and the engine noise from the German bombers. At night you could see the searchlights going up from Warley.

If the siren went while we were at school, we had to assemble in the big hall then we were led into the shelter. It was all done properly. We had to go marching in, carefully, not too quick. If we weren't at school, there was a public shelter on New Road but our mother wouldn't use it because a man had made advances towards her there and she was afraid to go back. We had an Anderson shelter in our garden but Mum didn't like going in there either because it was horrible and damp. There was a hole in the shelter for drainage but when it rained it got flooded and you wouldn't want to sleep in it. We only went in there when it was dry.

We weren't in the shelter when the Ursuline Convent School, which was right across the road from where we lived, got hit with incendiary bombs in December 1940. It went up in flames like a pile of matchsticks. The roof and the dormitories were badly damaged. We couldn't believe it. Me, my brother and my sister all went upstairs to watch it burning from our mother's bedroom window.

Anyway, all of the sudden there was a big knock on the door. It was the air raid warden and he was not happy. He could see me and my brother and sister standing there watching the fire. It was well ablaze. The warden got cross with my mum. He started swearing and god knows what. He was furious. He couldn't believe Mum was just letting us watch while the school went up. It was dangerous, I suppose. You could feel the heat through our windows. They might have exploded at any minute. But only the warden was frightened about it. We kids thought it was all good fun. We'd never seen anything like that fire before and we couldn't take our eyes off it. We were all just saying to each other, 'Cor, look at that!'

I think Woolworths on the High Street was hit the same night as the Ursuline. A month after that, a high explosive bomb destroyed some terraced houses near there. We'd walk past them on the way to school. It was fascinating to us kids. I went with my friends to collect shrapnel from the wreckage later on.

Around the same time, a German plane was shot down by an RAF Hurricane and crashed in nearby Hartswood. All the crew were killed. Later in the war, two American B-17 bombers collided in mid-air killing 19 men. I remember hearing about that.

One thing I remember about the war is that we were always starving hungry. There were shortages of food. Our grandfather shot rabbits to add to our rations. They were full of shot. Our uncle Alec used to catch rabbits with a snare, which was better.

One particular night I had a really vivid dream about eating a cake. It was so vivid that when I woke up, I went downstairs and looked everywhere to see if there was a cake hidden somewhere. I was sure I couldn't have imagined it. Of course there was nothing at all because everything was on rations and there was nothing to be had.

Our ration books were registered at a 'have it all' shop on Coptfold Road. It wasn't just a grocer's. They had sweets and all that too. The shop was owned by Mr Cross. Mum used to work for him, cleaning his house at the back of the shop, and he treated us well. He always helped Mum. He didn't give her extra but he always made sure we had enough. We were never rich. We were just an ordinary family.

Over the course of the war, lots of different troops came to train at Warley Barracks. There were Dutch soldiers and Polish airmen but the ones we were most interested in were the Americans - United States Army Air Forces from Willingdale Aerodrome at North Weald. The Americans parked some of their lorries in a car park on New Road, which was just around the corner from us.

We saw the Americans all the time. They'd come up to the High Street to go to the cinema. There was a big Odeon there then, with balconies and a circle and a restaurant upstairs. On Saturday mornings, we kids would go to watch cartoons. In the evenings, the American troops would go there. They had dances too.

We were really interested in the Americans' PX stores. PX stood for Post Exchange. The PX store for the Americans in Brentwood was in a church hall. It had a beautiful parquet floor but that was covered up to protect it while the hall was being used by the GIs. They had everything in there. Coca-Cola, bubble-gum, chewing gum...

We weren't shy of the Americans. In actual fact, I'd say we pestered them. We were always asking, 'Have you got any gum, chum?' And they usually had. They were very friendly and generous to us kids. No doubt about it. The best thing was when they gave us freshly cooked donuts from the PX, still warm. They were delicious. What they didn't give us, we pinched.

The American lorries were in a car park that backed on to an alleyway. It had an armed guard on the entrance and was surrounded by a chain link fence with barbed wire on the top. We couldn't climb over but the chain link didn't go right to the ground and we could get under it. The blackout helped us get in and out unseen.

Most of the lorries had canvas covers over the back, which were tied on with straps. They were easy to get into. Inside, there were bench seats. You could lift them up to get to the boxes underneath. We found lots of goodies that way. Once, we lifted up a bench seat and found dozens of tins of fruit. Big catering tins. I took a tin of peaches. When I got in, my mother asked, 'Where d'you get these from?' I told her I'd found them and she didn't push me to tell her where. She was just happy to have them.

Another night, me and my best friend Michael Whitty got into the back of a truck and found gum under one bench seat. Under the other bench seat was a box of balloons. We thought that was funny. What did the Yanks need balloons for? We took ourselves a box full.

On the way down Alfred Road, we stopped and tried to blow some of them up but no matter how hard we tried, we couldn't do it. These funny balloons kept slipping all over the place. We couldn't understand it.

The houses in Alfred Road had front gardens and there were a few adults outside enjoying the warm evening. When they saw me and Michael coming down the street, trying to blow those stupid balloons up, they all fell about laughing. Because of course the adults knew they weren't balloons at all. They were condoms!

In the end, Michael's father came out and took the condoms away from us. I don't know what he did with them. He was a Catholic.

We didn't ever get told off for what we'd been up to but the Americans must have noticed the boxes were gone.

Ahead of the Normandy landings, lots of troops came through Brentwood on their way to the coast. I think the Americans were hiding some of their armoured vehicles in the woods around the town so that the Germans couldn't see them if they flew overhead.

Then one morning in June 1944, we woke up to discover that all the Americans were gone. They'd just vanished overnight. Their lorries were gone from the car park. Their PX store had been packed up and closed down. We never saw them again. I suppose they must have all gone off for D-Day. We'd miss them.

Brentwood suffered badly with the V1s and V2s in 1944. I saw a doodlebug – a V1 flying bomb – come over. It came right over our house, tail burning, straight into Alfred Road and kept going.

When it was out of sight, we heard it stop and down it came. We had to go to the shelter after that.

The V2s – the rockets – were worse. You couldn't hear them at all. We only knew that London was getting it badly.

We heard that the war was over from Mum. She'd heard the news on the radio.

We had a party on our street for VE Day. Most of the men were still away in the forces so it was organised by the women. They clubbed together to do something nice for the children. They brought out all the food they had spare. I remember having corned beef sandwiches. The corned beef was Fray Bentos and came out of a tin with a little key that you had to turn round and round to get it open. I don't think it was on the ration. We had jelly too with some sort of cream, though I don't think it was real cream. It came out of a bottle. We had paper hats but nobody dressed up. I've got a photo of that day and you can see that the women all have their aprons on. We didn't have 'best' clothes, because clothing was on ration. We had to wear the same thing every day. There was music and we played games. We all had a jolly good time. Especially with all the food.

We celebrated again on VJ Day in August. We kids decided that we needed a bonfire and started to build one on Alfred Road. Some of the men were home again by then and they were all in the pub, celebrating with a drink. When they came out they saw what we'd been doing and told us, 'That bonfire ain't big enough.' They decided we needed their help and soon everyone on the street was involved, bringing out their broken old furniture to chuck on the top.

While this was going on, the police came round and told us that we couldn't light the bonfire because by now it was too big and might be dangerous. There was a blacksmith on Alfred Road, his name was Mr Porter. He ended up coming to the rescue. We moved the bonfire to his yard and were able to light it there. The bonfire burned all day, right up until we had to go to bed.

It should have been the start of a happy time but when Dad came home, he and Mum split up. They'd both become involved with other people while he was away. He ended up having a second family and didn't want to have much to do with us after that.

Our uncle Alec had been in Italy with the army. He fought in the Battle of Anzio in 1944. He had a terrible time and even though he came home he was never the same again.

After the war was over, we used to play in the Anderson shelter. We made it into a sort of den. Then one day the council turned up and took it away. And that was that.

22

D-DAY

AFTER NEARLY FIVE YEARS OF war with Germany, on June 6th 1944, henceforth known as D-Day, the pushback began in earnest as the Allied forces launched Operation Overlord: a coordinated assault, by land, sea and air, on Nazi-occupied France, with the aim of opening up a second front.

For days beforehand, the Allies had watched the weather, hoping for a break in stormy conditions. That break came early on June 6th, when the first Allied troops were parachuted into Northern France. Shortly afterwards, ground troops landed on five Normandy beaches, codenamed Gold, Utah, Omaha, Juno and Sword.

They were met with fierce resistance from the Germans but by the end of the day, a foothold had been established.

D-Day would go down in history. However for 14-year-old Doreen Dancer, whose two brothers were among the British troops landed in Normandy on that day, it was a moment of great anxiety. As the news began to report Allied successes and Allied casualties, Doreen could only hope she would see her brothers again.

Doreen Dancer, 95

THERE WERE SIX CHILDREN IN my family: four girls and two boys. I was evacuated with my two older sisters the day before war broke out. We went to Dorking, Surrey, to stay in an Edwardian mansion called Hurtwood House. I think it's a private school now. I remember clearly the moment war was declared. We were all gathered around the wireless and the adults were saying, 'be quiet, be quiet. The prime minister's coming on.' Chamberlain made the announcement – he had a very gruff voice – and some of the women fell straight to their knees and started crying. I wondered what was wrong with them. I didn't really know what war was.

We weren't at Hurtwood House for long. My sister Margaret got an abscess in her ear so we were sent to a nursing home in Shamley Green. I celebrated my 10th birthday there at the beginning of October. I've still got the New Testament the matron gave me as a birthday present. Then Dad came down to visit us and my oldest sister told him she wasn't happy. She didn't like being away from her friends. So he brought us all home again, to the estate on Garratt Lane in Wandsworth where we'd lived since 1938 when it was just finished and brand new.

We were in London all through the Blitz. There was a communal shelter on the estate but we only went down there once before Mum said, 'No. I'm not going in there anymore.' She couldn't stand it. Some of the women in the shelter couldn't take the stress of being bombed. Whenever they heard a bomb drop, they'd get down on their knees and start crying and praying and kicking up a fuss. They just couldn't take it but the way they went on made it worse for everybody else.

My mum was determined not to go in the shelter and Dad was happy with us all being at home during the air-raids too. We'd just get under the kitchen table. He said, 'if we go, we go together.'

Dad was working for Wandsworth Council at that time but he did fire-watching at the Corona drinks factory several nights a week. One night a bomb landed near us and a neighbour said, 'It's the Corona.' My sister Maisie went flying out to find him and Mum sent me running after her. When we found Dad, he had a window frame round his neck, like something out of a cartoon. He was cut and bruised but not too badly.

Another night, a nearby blast blew all our windows open and poor old Peter, our pet budgie, flew away in all the chaos.

Around the same time, Mum went to work for the first time. Having had six children, she'd stayed at home to look after us, but now that we were all older, she was able to go and work in a parachute factory. She liked it because she was earning money. She'd never earned her own money before.

I didn't go to school in any proper way during the war but I knew how to read and write because I'd learned my basics at Worple Way primary school before war broke out.

In the evenings we listened to *Children's Hour* and *ITMA*. The catchphrases stayed with you. There was a show where you could call in with messages for loved ones overseas. I liked that too. Our wireless set was funny. It had a little man, a diver, in a jar on it. I suppose it was a sort of valve or aerial. I remember hearing Princess Elizabeth's first speech to the nation. 'To children everywhere...'

I read the *Beano* and the *Dandy*, which were both pretty new. One of my favourite characters in the *Beano* was *Pansy Potter the Strongman's Daughter*. From time to time we went to the Savoy cinema. I liked to watch the organ rise up in front of the screen. I loved watching romances best of all. Hedy Lamarr and Greta Garbo were favourites.

When it came to keeping us children entertained, the Salvation Army were very good during the war. They used to come round with their band and let us play with the tambourines and the triangles. There wasn't much going on over Christmas in those days but the Salvation Army had lovely Christmas parties. I've still got a soft spot for them because of that.

As well as my three sisters, I had two brothers, George and Johnny, who were conscripted in 1944. They were both working in engineering when they got the telegrams to say, 'Report to so-and-so.' It must have been dreadful.

George and Johnny both went to France on D-Day and actually met up very briefly in Normandy. George had heard that John's regiment was ahead of his own and asked to be allowed to go and see him. They were both so young. John only turned 18 the day after D-Day.

For months, we didn't know what had happened to John after he and George said 'goodbye' on the beach. In August 1944, we had a letter from his Lieutenant Colonel saying that he was sure John was alright because he hadn't had official notice of his death. Lots of soldiers in John's regiment had been killed but his wasn't among the bodies they'd accounted for. But we knew that wasn't the same as a guarantee that John had made it through the fighting alive.

It was terrible for my parents, the not-knowing. Dad went to the war office every day to see if they had any news of him but they just kept saying, 'We don't know where he is, Mr Hancock. We haven't heard a thing.' I carried on writing to John myself but the letters went undelivered. They were found somewhere in Germany after the war ended and got sent back to me.

We eventually found out what had happened to John when we received a letter out of the blue from a young woman called Tanya, who said she was a nurse in Paris.

'Dear Mrs Hancock,' she wrote to my mother. 'I've been looking after your baby boy.'

You can imagine how it felt for us to hear that news. We were all so excited.

I always assumed Tanya was French but a neighbour thought that with her name she might be Russian and told us we should be careful. 'There's a war going on and you don't know who this person is.' We didn't care who she was. She'd been looking after our John, who'd been wounded in battle and ended up a prisoner of war. We wrote straight back to her to find out more. We ended up swapping lots of letters, Tanya and me.

We knew my brother George was alright because he'd sent a photo of himself in bed in a hospital. We don't know why he was there. George fought on into Germany and he was among the troops that liberated a concentration camp. I think that stayed with him for the rest of his life.

On VE Day, I went to Trafalgar Square and Hyde Park with some pals. From the top of the bus on our way into town we saw all sorts of street parties. There were crowds everywhere. We met up with a group of boys and had a wonderful evening, dancing and singing in the park. It was so rowdy. Though there was no hanky panky, you understand! It was different in those days. We never saw those boys again but for that one evening, everybody was the best of friends. We were elated that the war was over. It was wonderful.

My brothers were always very modest about what they did in the war but years later, when George died and his daughter Marion cleared his home, she found that he'd received a commendation from Field Marshal Montgomery. She also found a letter from a sergeant in the Black Watch, thanking George for saving his life. George had never talked about either of those things. He and John never told us anything about their time with the army in Europe. They didn't want to relive it and I don't blame them. We were just glad to have them both back.

23

VENGEANCE

Hitler Strikes Back

IF THERE WAS ONE THING the British had come to know about Hitler, it was that he was a great believer in revenge. Just a week after the Allied success that was D-Day, Hitler hit back by targeting British civilians with a new terror, one of his aptly named 'vengeance weapons' (Vergeltungswaffen) - the V1 Flying Bomb.

Even before the V1s reached London, they had been responsible for many thousands of deaths. The jet-powered winged bombs were created using slave labour from the Mittelbau-Dora concentration camp in Central Germany, where it's believed 20,000 prisoners were killed in the underground factories they were forced to build by tunnelling into the surrounding mountains.

The first V1 to reach Britain fell on a railway bridge over Grove Road in London's Bow at 4.30 in the morning on June 13th 1944, taking out the railway line from Liverpool Street station to Stratford. Six civilians were killed in the blast and a further 42 were injured.

Twelve houses were destroyed, leaving many more homeless. Baffled by the 'pilotless plane' found on the bridge and how it had got through Britain's air defences, Herbert Morrison, minister for Home Security, placed a temporary embargo on any mention of the incident in the press, so that the Germans might not know how successful their new weapon had been.

To the Nazis, the V1's were 'Wunderwaffe' or wonder weapons. To the British public, they quickly became known as 'buzz bombs' or 'doodlebugs', due to the curious buzzing noise they made in flight (Hitler had also called the bombs *Maikäfer* or May Bug for a while). No matter what they were called, everyone soon became acutely aware that when the buzzing stopped, that's when you were in trouble, as the V1 would then plummet pretty much straight to the ground. There was very little time to hide from a suddenly silent doodlebug and soon more than 100 a day were heading across the Channel.

To begin with the V1s were all programmed to make their way towards Tower Bridge but the Germans didn't care if they didn't reach their ultimate target, so long as they caused chaos on the way. Croydon was particularly unlucky, with many V1s finishing their journey prematurely in the town nine miles south of the capital.

Nothing like the V1s had ever been seen before but the army and RAF moved quickly to mitigate the problem. Along the south-east coast of England, the V1s met huge batteries of anti-aircraft guns which shot many V1s down long before they could reach their targets. Around 2,000 barrage balloons were sent up, in the hope that the V1s would become tangled in their tethers. That worked until the edges of the V1s wings were equipped with blades that could cut through wire.

Daring Allied fighter pilots in Mosquitoes and Spitfires even engaged with the V1s in mid-air, having discovered that they could 'tip' them with their wings, causing them bombs to drop from the sky and land safely in the sea. Of the 8,000 V1s launched towards London, many were brought down by balloons, guns and sheer bravado. Others didn't make it to launch, thanks to the heroic prisoners at Dora-Mittlebau who sabotaged many of the rockets they were forced to produce (200 members of that incredibly brave organised prisoner resistance group were hanged). However many more V1s got through Allied defences to cause havoc. Such as happened one sunny morning in Clapham in July 1944, when war baby Vivienne Rhodes was just a few weeks old.

Vivienne Rhodes, 81

I WAS BORN EARLY IN 1944. My parents were living in Clapham at the time but for my birth, as for the births of my two big sisters before me, Mum was taken to St Albans, where a temporary maternity hospital had been created at the Bishop's Palace, Verulam House, for those mothers-to-be who would otherwise have gone to the General Lying In Hospital in London.

At the outbreak of war my father – then 19 – had straightaway joined the army but, because he was very good at maths, he was seconded to the War Office where he ended up working in the accounting department. Apparently, he got some snooty reactions from the neighbours who looked down on him because he hadn't been sent to the front.

My parents had been to the same school in Larkhall Lane in Stockwell but because Dad was two years older, they didn't really know each other until they met again socially after they'd both left. They were married in 1940, shortly before the birth of my eldest sister Wendy.

To begin with, Mum and Dad lived with Mum's parents on Edgeley Road until they were able to afford to move into a flat of their own on Lynette Avenue. That was where we were living four years later when a V1 fell between our row of houses and the street behind.

It happened one sunny July morning. By sheer luck, none of us were at home. By this time, Dad was away training with the army ahead of going overseas and Mum had taken me and my sisters to our grandparents' house. When she got back to Lynnette Avenue that afternoon, she was astonished to see what looked like our wardrobe on the other side of the road. The bomb blew it clean out of our flat.

I can't imagine how awful it must have been to realise how close the war had come to our little family but Mum was pragmatic. Neighbours helped her to gather up some personal belongings, then she took me and my two sisters – me still a babe in arms and my sisters both under four – to the shelter at Clapham South Tube Station. Mum's eldest sister Mabel and her brother Arthur were both wardens there. It was the deepest shelter in London at the time and had been set aside for mothers and children. It could house 8,000 people when full and it was well-equipped by Tube shelter standards, with proper toilets and washing facilities. There was a medical station there too and a canteen but we stayed in the shelter for just one night before Mum bundled us all on a train bound for Buckinghamshire, to stay with Uncle Dan, who was a friend of my paternal grandfather.

We stayed in Buckinghamshire for about a week before we came back to London to see Dad who was on embarkation leave. We stayed with his parents at Narbonne Avenue for a few hectic days while Mum and Dad rescued more things from our old flat.

The blast on Lynnette Avenue must have brought home how dangerous it was to be in London at that time and not long afterwards my parents decided that we children would be altogether safer in the country. It was arranged that my sisters and I would be evacuated, with Mum because I was still so small, and Dad was given 48 hours leave to help organise the move.

For some reason, my big sister Wendy – still only four years old – was evacuated separately from the rest of us. She went, with a coachload of other small children, to Oakham in Rutland. However, she wasn't sent to live with a family. Instead, she was sent to a sort of boarding nursery, set up in a requisitioned house – it might have been Lord Lonsdale's house, which became the Barleythorpe Hall Home for Babies – where several children were cared for by professional nursing staff. The house was beautifully equipped, with everything a child might wish for – there were paddling pools and sandpits and lots of toys, donated by the American troops at the local airbase – but obviously the staff, while very kind, were no substitute for Mum and Dad and to this day Wendy wonders about the effects of the experience of being separated from the rest of us.

While Wendy was in Rutland, Mum, my sister Diane and I were sent to Chesterfield, a market town in Derbyshire. Mum knew nothing about the place, except that it was one of the names on her father's pool coupons.

We left London on a glorious summer's day. Dad was able to come with us, helping Mum and the other evacuees in our cohort with their luggage. When we arrived there, we were taken to the town hall. Dad had to go back to London, to work, and Mum was left to wait to see where we would be staying. That day in the town hall was like a slave market and by the end of the day, Mum was still waiting for someone to say they would take us on. A single man, with no family of his own, did offer us a place to stay, but Mum knew that Dad's answer to that would be 'not bloody likely'.

At the end of the day, we were still waiting to find a billet, when a lady arrived. She was married but had no children. Her husband wasn't with her that afternoon but she was in the company of a policeman – a friend of her husband's – who persuaded her to take us in. Mum remembers her saying, 'I don't know what Jack'll say about this.'

The lady's name was Eunice. Her husband Jack, a police sergeant, was away on a fishing trip when Eunice welcomed us into their home. She and Mum must have had a tense wait for Jack's return. When he did get home, he walked through the back door into the kitchen to find my sister Diane playing at the kitchen table and me, just a few months old and without a hair on my head, gurgling away as I lay in a drawer that was doubling for a cot.

As my mother always told the story, Jack, far from being upset that Eunice had moved a family into his house without asking, was transported upon seeing me and my angel-faced sister. He fell in love with us. He nicknamed me 'Sweet Pea' after the bald-headed baby in the *Popeye* cartoons.

Eunice and Jack became like family to us. My sisters and I called them Auntie and Uncle. Eunice was from Nottinghamshire, Jack from Yorkshire. They always had a pet dog and budgies.

Mum did her best not to make our presence in the house too tiresome for our kind hosts. It must have been hard dealing with our nappies in a strange house. My sister and I were potty trained pretty quickly!

Both Eunice and Jack went out to work, so Mum had the house to herself during the day. She did the housework to earn her keep and was very careful with Jack and Eunice's belongings, so she was mortified when, one lunchtime, my sister Diane threw a silver egg-cup across the kitchen, breaking it in two. Mum quickly loaded me and my sister into our pram and ran to catch the bus into town, where she had a jeweller solder the egg cup back together. When she admitted to Eunice that there had been an accident, Eunice was characteristically kind about the breakage, reassuring Mum that she really didn't mind. It was just a thing.

From time to time, when he was on leave, Dad would come and visit. To give Mum a break he would load us into our pram and push us around the village, which evidently set curtains twitching. Men didn't push prams in those days. But whatever the village gossips might have thought, Dad set a trend and soon men pushing prams was an everyday sight.

Mum visited Wendy in Rutland whenever she was able. I can't imagine how difficult it must have been for both of them – especially Wendy – when it was time to say goodbye.

The people who looked after Wendy were very kind and would write to Mum often to tell her how she was getting on. They told Mum that Wendy was a 'dear little girl' who always helped the others, even though she was very small herself. The head of the boarding nursery told Mum a story of a day when Wendy received a letter from us. She called Wendy in and told her, 'You've got a letter from Mummy. Would you like me to read it for you?' Of course Wendy said yes. The woman read the letter then Wendy asked this heart-breaking question: 'You will look after that letter, won't you?'

To add to the agony of separation, my other sister Diane contracted meningitis and was sent to a hospital in Sheffield to recover. While Mum shuttled between Sheffield and Rutland, my Granny Stockton came to visit. Luckily, she got on very well with Eunice. They became firm friends.

Diane was given a new drug which helped her to recover from meningitis more quickly than expected. Apparently, it helped that she was well-nourished. We certainly never went hungry. Eunice and Jack had a huge garden where they grew lots of soft fruits.

When it was time for Diane to come home, the WVS in Chesterfield supplied a car to go and fetch her, another example of the kindness and generosity of the town that had taken us in. Diane made a good recovery though she was left with hearing problems in one ear.

We were in Chesterfield for about a year. As soon as the war ended, Mum wanted to go straight back to London, so that Wendy could come home and we could all be together again. Since our home on Lynnette Avenue had not been rebuilt, we had to wait for new accommodation to be found. We ended up in the first floor flat in a grand house on Kings Avenue between Clapham and Tulse Hill. The huge bedroom, which I shared with my sisters, was painted blue with a frieze of butterflies floating around the walls. I've loved butterflies ever since.

Rationing continued long after the war but I don't ever think we went hungry. We ate lots of fish. I learned very young how to get the bones out of kippers. The only thing I really disliked eating was swedes. Perhaps it was the margarine they were cooked with. When we had butter, Mum would tell us we weren't allowed to put jam and butter on our bread at the same time, but should savour the taste of the butter and save the jam to cover the taste of the 'special' margarine.

In 1944, my father was sent to the Far East. He wasn't able to tell Mum exactly where he was going but she wrote to him all the time. She didn't tell him about Diane's meningitis until after he was home from the war, not wanting to worry him when he was so far away.

As far as we know, Dad went first to Egypt, then to India, before joining the fighting in Burma and ending up in Singapore.

Mum told me that while Dad was away, she sometimes found she would ask herself whether she would know him when he came home. Would the war have changed him beyond recognition? Dad was away for three years in the end, having stayed on in Singapore to work on rebuilding the administrative systems of the island. He was asked if he would like to have us brought over to join him but decided against it, since we were happily resettled in London by then.

I was less than a year old when Dad went away. When he came back to London I was three. I can still clearly remember the moment he came home. It was late at night. My sisters and I were in bed but Dad couldn't resist looking in on his girls. He slowly opened the door to the bedroom I shared with Wendy and Diane. Half-awake, I saw this enormous man-shaped shadow fill the door (in my memory he is wearing his bush hat) and screamed. I thought I was having a nightmare.

Having been so small when he went to the Far East, I hadn't had a chance to get to know my father at all but I soon got used to him. In fact, I was fascinated by him and would follow him around the house. I loved listening to him sing while he was shaving, though I picked up some very risqué songs, which I sang to my sisters without having any idea how rude the lyrics were.

When my sisters and I were growing up, we didn't think to ask Dad about his time in the Far East and he didn't like to tell us. He opened up more to his grandchildren, many decades later. He told one of my nephews that he had been a prisoner of war. He did have a scar on his arm that he claimed was a bullet wound. We do know that he must have contracted malaria while he was away because he suffered from occasional recurrences of the disease throughout his life.

Once he was demobbed, Dad went back to the civil service. My younger sister Heather was born in 1948 so Mum had her hands full at home. Shortly after she was born, we were given a council house in Streatham, a three-bedroom semi, with a garden. It was newly built on what had been a bomb site. I was overjoyed to have so much space and remember being thrilled when I asked Mum whether we could run up and down the stairs and was told that I could, now that we no longer had neighbours downstairs to worry about.

Though we had stayed in Chesterfield for only a year, we kept in touch with Auntie Eunice and Uncle Jack for many years to come. Wendy and Heather would come with me and Diane to stay in Chesterfield during the school holidays and they both found themselves very welcome there too. It remained our home from home. Uncle Jack continued to call me Sweet Pea, and that was the name he still called me years later, when he came to see me get married.

24

LONDON IN THE DOODLEBUG SUMMER

'Please don't let it come down...'

THE RELENTLESS DOODLEBUG ATTACKS OF 1944 exacted an enormous psychological toll. It wasn't only London that the Germans targeted with the horrifying weapons that could be fired by day or night. Southampton, Portsmouth and Greater Manchester also suffered. The random nature of the attacks terrified many more people into fleeing Britain's cities. But in the summer of 1944 one young Londoner made the opposite journey, preferring to take her chances with the doodlebugs over the isolation of life as an evacuee in rural Wales.

Though Viv Rhodes was too young to remember the V1 that changed her life, Beryl Morgan was old enough to know exactly what it meant when a doodlebug's engine cut out, as happened when she was gazing out of her bedroom window at one of Britain's most important public buildings. Behind the Tate Britain, one of London's most famous art galleries, was a housing estate of buildings named after famous artists. That's where Beryl's family lived during the war, in the block named after JMW Turner.

Beryl Morgan, 93

WHEN THE WAR STARTED, I was evacuated along with my older sister, Mary. She was at a private school – she'd won a scholarship – and the school arranged for her and a group of her classmates to be sent to stay with a titled lady near Tunbridge Wells. I understood that this lady, whom we called Lady Payne, was a cousin of the Queen. I wasn't at the same school as Mary but my parents asked if I could go with her, because I was the youngest in the family and didn't want to be evacuated somewhere else on my own. Lady Payne agreed.

Lady Payne didn't get too involved with us evacuees. We only met her a couple of times. We had a sort of school mistress looking after us. But it was very nice. We had a wing of the house to ourselves. I shared a bedroom with Mary and we could have a bath every night. Mary was six or seven years older than me so she was in charge of making sure I had my bath. It was usually too hot but she wouldn't take any notice of me. Because she wanted to be a nurse, she'd test it with her elbow and tell me not to be silly. She was very business-like. I had to go to bed at seven, but Mary and the other girls could stay up later.

Lady Payne had a cook and a gardener. The cook used to dish up our meals. I remember one day finding a worm in the cabbage I'd been given for my dinner. The school mistress called the cook and she took the worm away but left the cabbage with me. Then the school mistress said, "Carry on eating." But I didn't want to. Nothing could persuade me. When I refused, she told Mary to give me a bath and put me straight to bed. It was only about three o'clock in the afternoon. It was the longest night. I was thinking when's the morning going to come?

I turned seven while we were at Lady Payne's and I was taken on a day-trip to a nearby house – it looked like a castle to me. Perhaps it was Hever Castle. Later that day I had a party of sorts, with another little girl and boy who were staying with us. They must have been brother and sister. All I can remember is that the two of them had their bath together and the little boy said, 'Pass the soap, Marjorie,' in a very posh accent. I don't know why that's stayed with me more than the party!

There were no small children back at the house so I often bothered the gardener for company. He would show me the greenhouses, where he grew tomatoes and grapes. Lady Payne donated the grapes to convalescents at the local hospital. I remember that once, when I was out in the garden, the gardener came chasing after me for a joke and I fell over, getting a stone stuck in my knee. Lady Payne's two sons took me to hospital in the back of their soft-top sports car. They stayed with me while the doctor sorted my knee out.

Both sons joined the forces and, unfortunately, one of them was killed. Shortly after that, we evacuees were moved elsewhere. I don't know whether it's because, in her grief, Lady Payne didn't want to have lots of children around her, or if the house was requisitioned for something else. All I know is that a man came to find me at school and told me I must meet my sister afterwards, because we were going to a place called Hever Warren Farm. That was it. We didn't get a chance to say 'goodbye' or 'thank you' to Lady Payne. We didn't see any of the other girls again either. But I loved Hever Warren Farm. It was absolute bliss to be there because I was mad about animals.

The brother and sister who ran the farm were very kind to us but the local children weren't friendly, as if they thought we'd invaded their patch in some way. They probably thought that if someone comes from London, they're going to be a bully. I didn't mind too much because I was so happy on the farm. They had dairy cows and a great big bull. I did learn how to milk a cow. One of my favourite pranks was to hide the farmer's milking stool. Looking back, that must have been very annoying.

The farm also had chickens. There was one rooster in particular who made an impression because whenever I came home from school, he would be waiting. As soon as he saw me he'd fly at me! I'd try to find another way to get in but he'd always find me somehow. It was terrible.

I don't know how long we stayed at the farm, but soon Mary was old enough to leave school and train as a nurse and for that she had to go to London. I was still only seven so even though I loved being on the farm and the people there said they'd look after me, I thought I ought to go back home.

When Mary and I reappeared at home, my mother asked me, 'What did you want to come back here for?'

She had a point. Westminster was heavily bombed in the Blitz. The block we lived in had been hit while I was away and a number of people had died. It happened on May 11th 1941. A 1,000lb bomb dropped on the opposite side of the buildings from us and they were so badly damaged my mother had to let the rescue teams climb through my bedroom window to get in to rescue the casualties. The only damage to our flat was that a bomb blast had blown the door off.

My friend's mother, a lovely Irish woman, was caught up in that bomb. She was the last to be dug out of the rubble. Mum told me she had asked for a cuppa while she was waiting to be rescued and they had given her a sponge soaked in tea. She didn't make it.

There was a shelter in our building but Mum wouldn't ever go into it because she didn't like to leave our dog Prince alone in the flat. Prince was only a tiny little thing but animals weren't allowed. She'd start whining as soon as she heard the siren and Mum couldn't bear to leave her behind. Mum was brave to risk her life like that.

I wasn't back in Westminster for long before my school was evacuated again. When we left London, we didn't have any idea where we were going. We ended up in Wales.

I was billeted with some nice people but I wasn't happy because the wife wouldn't let me go out to play. The other evacuees would knock and say, 'Can Beryl come over the park?' but she always said 'no'. I used to have to walk the family's baby, her name was Wendy, up and down outside the house instead.

Then one day, I was walking in the village when I heard the unmistakable sound of a Cockney accent. I went up to the woman I'd heard talking and asked if she was from London. She told me she was and she was going back the following week. I begged her to take me too but, of course, I had to ask my mother.

I wrote a letter that night. 'Please, please, send me the money for the fare. This lady's going to bring me home.' Mum wrote back and told me no because the bombing was too heavy. The Cockney woman agreed with my mother. But Mum must have thought about it because a day later she sent the fare. I was delighted. Looking back, I can see it wasn't fair to the woman that had taken me in. When I told her I was going home, she said, 'Well, all the evacuees are getting new boots and new Mackintoshes. You're going to lose out on all of that.'

I didn't care. I wanted to be back in London. The Cockney lady took me home and Mum was sort of grateful but once again she told me, 'You're silly because the bombs are still dropping.'

I was glad to be back and among my friends. Mum at least used to let me play out. Whips and tops were popular. We'd chalk patterns on the tops to see them turn into a sort of kaleidoscope while they were spinning. We loved skating too. Well, if we could find skates. I had one. It was a left one but I used to put it on my right foot to try to balance things out. That was the extent of our play equipment. We had to make our own games up really. But on

Saturdays, we would go to the Biograph cinema in Wilton Road. It was 10d to get in. On the way home we'd buy 2d worth of chips smothered in vinegar and that was our treat. Looking back we were quite content.

Though Mum never went into the shelter, I did. It was inside the building. They'd reinforced an area of the bottom floor with planks. I don't know how sturdy it was. It was very loud in there when a raid was going on. You could hear the planes going over and the shrapnel dropping. I was so frightened. The adults were all talking and trying to cheer one another up, saying, 'It's gone, it's gone.' They were pretty calm but whenever you heard a crash, you thought, 'are we next?' That's an awful feeling.

I heard later that when the Blitz started, there was one woman in our building who lost it every time there was a raid and the way she carried on was so upsetting, lots of people didn't want to be in the shelter with her. That might have been the reason why there were so many casualties when the Turner buildings did get hit in 1941.

In 1944, the V1s – the doodlebugs – arrived. This is God's truth: I was in my bedroom, which overlooked the Tate. I looked up and saw a doodlebug coming over. They always said that when it's whistling, it's fine, but when it stops... So I was watching this doodlebug and saying to myself, 'Please don't let it drop here.' I was whispering, 'Please, please don't let it stop here, please, don't let it come down.' And it stopped whistling right over the gallery. I was terrified. But somehow it carried on over the gallery, over our building and landed on the other side. I think it took out a lot of shops.

Then came the V2s. You got no warning with the V2s at all. They just suddenly came down. That was terrifying. The Germans didn't lose any men sending them, did they?

Dad was too old to be called up. He worked for Westminster Council during the day and by night he was an air raid warden with the ARP. He worked alongside one of Churchill's daughters – Sarah, I think it was. He told me she was a good laugh and was always up for joining the rest of the team at the pub at the end of a shift.

Dad was very brave. While I was in the shelter, he had to be out in the raids. Once he was called to a house where some blind people were living. The street had been hit and the roof of their house was coming in so Dad had to get them out. They were refusing to leave, saying, 'Where's the cat? Where's the cat?' Dad couldn't see any cat but he told them, 'The cat's already got out,' just to get the people moving.

Dad was involved in protecting the Tate Gallery too. They'd moved most of the artwork out to safe-keeping in the countryside and down in some of the Tube stations but the building was still vulnerable. Dad told me a story about one night, when the bombing was particularly bad, and all London was burning. Because the fire brigade was busy elsewhere, Dad had to deal with putting out a small fire at the Tate on his own. Someone from the fire brigade handed Dad a hose and he got to work. But the thing is, once he'd put out the fire, there was no-one to turn the hose off. Dad couldn't put the hose down and turn it off himself because the water jet was so forceful, if Dad let go the hose would swing and might even break his legs. So he just had to stand there, hanging on to the hose for dear life, waiting for reinforcements!

That was one of Dad's funny stories but his ARP work must have taken a toll. He wasn't given to crying but I remember he did cry after the disaster at Balham Station, when a water main burst and flooded the shelter there. The only other time I saw him cry was when my sister Rosie died.

As well as Mary, the sister I was evacuated with, I had two other sisters. Jessie was the oldest. She was already married and had left home. Rosie came between me and Mary. Rosie wasn't evacuated to Kent because she had a weak heart. She went to Chessington, where they had set up a school with hospital facilities for children that needed that sort of care.

Rosie got through the war. She got married and had a baby – Janet – but because her heart was weak, she was warned that she shouldn't have another. When Janet was born, Rosie was living in Rotherhithe. She hated it there. She had to go out shopping in the fog one day and contracted pneumonia. She died on her way to hospital. Janet was only nine months old.

At the end of the war, we had a party on the estate. The different buildings each had their own little party but pretty soon we had all joined together, making one big table. All the children had paper hats and there was lots to eat because people had had an idea that the war was coming to an end and they had saved up their rations.

The following year, I left school at 14 and went to work in an architect's office in Victoria. I remember once as I was walking home, I saw this big car, with a soldier driving it. As it went by, the passenger waved and I realised it was Monty – Field Marshal Montgomery. He had a flat on Marsham Street. I didn't wave back because I thought Monty couldn't possibly have been waving at me but after he was gone, I looked behind me and realised that there was no-one else around so he must have been waving to me after all!

After Mary completed her nursing training, she met her husband, a submariner, in the hospital where she was working. They went off to New Zealand. Before she went, she and I went back to visit Hever Warren Farm. They had all the Land Army girls there. I didn't keep in touch with our foster family, which was a shame because they were really, really lovely people.

My eldest sister Jessie's husband Reggie had joined the army at the beginning of the war and was sent to Crete, along with two of his brothers: Billy and Johnny. As soon as they landed, they realised the Germans were waiting for them on the beach. Unfortunately, Reggie and Johnny were already off the boat by then. Billy managed to escape but Reggie and Johnny were taken prisoner and kept in a POW camp for the rest of the war. They had to work on a farm and were barely given anything to eat.

The camp Reggie and Johnny were in was liberated by the Americans. They gave the POWs lots of German memorabilia. Reggie came home with a German helmet. But he had been malnourished in the camp and he also came home with tuberculosis. He was very ill, so he was taken straight to a military hospital. They wanted to do an operation on him to relieve his symptoms – it would have involved taking a rib out. Reggie wouldn't let them do it and he died.

After Jessie was widowed, I would go and stay with her, to keep her company for a while. Once, she said, 'Come and meet my new boyfriend.' I went along and was astonished to meet this lovely Jamaican man. Through him I met my husband Steve, who was also Jamaican. He came to England just after the Windrush. We fell in love and he asked me to marry him. My parents were shocked. It wasn't done in those days to marry someone of a different race. At first my mother said she wasn't going to come to the wedding, but she did. She understood that I loved him and she wanted me to be happy. That's all it takes, isn't it? Steve was a very kind mind with a big work ethic. We had five children and now I've got 12 grandchildren and five great-grandchildren. They all look after me.

The war changed everybody's lives. It changed the directions we went in for bad and for good. It's strange to think that if poor Reggie hadn't got TB in the POW camp and my sister hadn't been widowed, I might never have met Steve.

I do think it made my generation more resilient. We tended to get on with it. We had to. It's quite something when you think about it, isn't it? You see wars going on now on the TV news and then remember that we were living that kind of existence; waiting for the bombs to drop, not knowing what was going to happen next.

25

A SILENT MENACE

The V2s

JUST AS BRITAIN WAS GETTING used to the V1s, Hitler revealed that he still had another card up his sleeve.

The V1s were bad enough, subjecting British civilians to a horrible game of musical shelters. When the noise stopped, would you be close enough to safety to live to play the game another day? But with the V1s, you at least had something of a warning in the terrible sound of their engines. Nobody could hear the V2s coming.

Hitler's hugely expensive new toy was a rocket as tall as a house, fuelled by a mixture of ethanol and liquid oxygen. Upon being launched it would fly all the way to the edge of the earth's atmosphere before plummeting back to Earth at unthinkable speed. While the V1s had a limited range and had to be launched from sites in Northern France or the Netherlands, or from modified Heinkel He 111 aircraft, to hit the south of England, the V2s had no such restrictions. They were the world's first long-range ballistic missiles.

London saw its first V2 on the evening of September 8th 1944, when a rocket fired all the way from Wassenaar in the Netherlands landed in Staveley Road, Chiswick, near the junction with Burlington Lane. It killed three people, including a three-year-old girl, and injured 22 more. It left an enormous crater, more than six metres deep. Eleven houses had to be demolished and more than 550 others were damaged. The disruption was enormous.

Just as with the first V1, news of the attack was carefully managed in an attempt to keep the Germans from knowing that their missile had made it through British air defences. Local people were told that a gas main had exploded. They would be kept in the dark for two months.

It's believed that the V1s and V2s combined caused more than 30,000 civilian casualties, while leaving many more homeless. Ironically, the manufacturing of the V weapons proved even more deadly than their deployment. But that was no consolation to the people of Hazlehurst Road, childhood home of Maud Smith, which was hit by a V2 on the morning of Sunday November 19th 1944.

Maud Smith, 93

I WAS ABOUT SEVEN WHEN the war began. I had two brothers and the older of the two, Stan, and I were staying with our grandmother because Mum was in hospital with septic peritonitis. She almost lost her life. My younger brother was still a baby so a neighbour was looking after him. Dad was away with the Navy.

After war was declared, there were a few false alarm air raid signals, which left Nan fearing for our lives. She couldn't cope with the worry, so she put me and Stan on a train, care of the guard, and sent us to stay with our Aunt Kit, who lived in Bradford On Avon in Wiltshire. Aunt Kit's house was posh. Must have been because she had a tablecloth! I shared a room with my cousin Pat while Stan shared a room with Pat's brother Peter. We all got on well. I picked up my love of reading at Aunt Kit's house. They were always absorbed in books.

I remember that every bedtime, Pat would kneel down beside the bed and say her prayers. I found that fascinating. Pat got me to go to church on a Sunday, which I loved. I hadn't often been to church in London, but I found I loved the solitude and peace. Most of all I liked getting away from my noisy brothers.

I'm not sure how long we stayed at Aunt Kit's but Mum was in hospital for quite a while. At one point they thought she might lose her life and Dad was given compassionate leave to come home and see her. Years later, I found out that Mum had contracted septic peritonitis through a self-abortion. With Dennis still so small and war on the horizon, she just couldn't see how she could look after another child.

At the time, Stan and I were too young to know what was going on at home. We were enjoying being in the countryside. The weather was really severe that winter of 1939. Aunt Kit lived near a farm and when we walked through the fields we would make sure to break the ice on the water troughs for the animals.

It was so cold that the canal that ran between Bradford On Avon and Trowbridge froze over. When that happened, people would use the frozen canal as a shortcut, skating from town to town. That was great fun. But one day, one of the teachers at the local school lost her life when the ice broke beneath her. That brought home how risky it was.

I did go to school in Wiltshire but I have much clearer memories of the things we did on our days off. I can remember helping the local milkman. He didn't have bottles. He had a barrow on which he wheeled a big milk churn about the streets and people would come out with their own jugs to be filled.

We were at Aunt Kit's for most of the winter but as soon as Mum came out of hospital, we went home. She was better but still very weak so she needed a lot of help. I'm sure Stan and I were glad to be home but it wasn't long before the bombs started falling.

We lived on Hazlehurst Road in Wandsworth then, next to a yard where they kept horses and donkeys. When the bombers were flying over, the horses would go crazy, kicking at their stable doors so that we could hear them. I was frightened enough without that. Then one day I heard that my school was organising an expedition of evacuees and I asked if I could join them. Mum agreed that Stan and I could go but Dennis was still too small.

This time, we went to Devon. Lots of other children we knew from London were there too and we were happy to have friends nearby. We stayed with a woman called Mrs Nutt. Most evacuees called the adults they stayed with 'aunt' or 'uncle' but Mrs Nutt was so old I called her 'gran'.

The Nutts had a big garden where they grew lots of fruit and veg. I loved to go down there and pick raspberries straight off the canes, ready to have with cream at teatime. I can still remember the very first time I tasted Devon cream. I was so sick! It was much too rich for me but I soon developed a taste for it.

We must have been in Devon for about a year before we came back to London again. By this time, we had moved from Hazlehurst Road to be closer to my grandmother in Upper Tooting. Gran found a place for us to rent in Hereward Road. It was in a pretty poor state, having been empty for several years before we moved in. There were lots of empty houses about because people were off at the war or getting out of the city.

This was the time of the V1s. They really frightened me. You'd hear the noise of the engine and when it stopped, you had to take cover, throw yourself into a hedge, whatever. When the air raid sirens sounded, sometimes we just got under the table. Once or twice I went down into the underground at Tooting Broadway but there were so many people down there it was horrible. Other times I went with some of the older girls I knew to a shelter in the cellar under Cedar's the menswear shop but I contracted scabies from the blankets.

We went to the baths once a week. We had a tin bath at home but now that I was growing up I wanted privacy. There was no bathroom at home. Our house was old-fashioned. We still had gas lighting. There was definitely no central heating. To stay warm, we had to sit with our feet on the fender. Mice would come running out when the fire was lit.

I remember hearing one bomb fall really nearby. We didn't have time to go to the shelter so Mum pulled me into a cupboard under the stairs. I screamed so loud! I wasn't frightened of the bombs but I was frightened of the rats that were under the stairs with us. Rats used to come into the house from the sewer. I hated them. They were so nasty and huge. They killed our cat. Added to that, the ceilings in our house had started falling all around us because the rats had been eating the joists. There was dust all over the place from where the bomb blast had shaken our house.

When the raid was over, it was clearing up time. There was always so much work to be done and I ended up doing most of it because Mum had a bad heart. I don't know why she didn't call me Cinderella.

I couldn't go out unless I'd finished my chores. When I did go out to play, it was to join the other children in the debris in the middle of the road. That was our playground. At school, all the classrooms were sandbagged so that the windows wouldn't break onto us if there was a bomb. We still took our classes as usual. At assembly we sang as if there wasn't a war on.

It was a good job we moved from Hazlehurst Road when we did. At half eight in the morning, on Sunday November 19th 1944, the road was hit by a V2 rocket that destroyed half the houses, killing 34 people and injuring 100 more. There were 14 children among the dead. One was a baby, just six months old.

On the Monday, after school, me and some of my schoolmates went to see the bombsite. What a terrible scene greeted us on the road where we used to play. I couldn't believe what had happened. The Red Cross was still there and the fire brigade and the police. They were still dragging out bodies and bits of bodies, arms and legs... It was horrible. I'll never forget it. I'll never get the horror of it out of my mind. I wished we hadn't gone to look.

Later, we heard that one of our former neighbours had come home from work that day to discover that he'd lost his wife and seven children. I was only 11 and it really scared me. The minute I heard there was going to be another evacuation expedition from school, I asked to go.

The third time I was evacuated, Mum sent both my brothers with me and we went to Leicestershire. Though you hoped you were going to safety, being evacuated was always a traumatic event. You've got your gas mask and you're told to go along with the group but you don't know where you're going and when you get to your destination, you're all herded into a hall and have to wait for the foster families to turn up and choose you, like a cattle market.

Before we left London, Mum told me, 'Whatever happens, don't be separated from your younger brother.' She meant Dennis, who was still only four. Anyway, we got to Leicester and were taken to this school hall to wait for the people who were going to take us home.

All these people came in and one by one the children we'd arrived with were taken off to live with various families until there was just me and my two brothers left. No-one wanted to take on three children at once. Then this little girl – she was about my age – came up to me and said, 'My mum wouldn't mind an evacuee.' I had to tell her, 'I can't come unless you have my baby brother too.' I hoped they'd take Stan as well. The little girl, whose name was Mary, told me, 'I'll have to ask.' She came back with her mum a few minutes later, who agreed to take me and Dennis but not Stan. I suppose she only had room for two and thought Stan would get taken home by someone else.

That afternoon, Dennis and I went home with Mary and her mum – Mrs Vestey – but we had to leave Stan behind in the hall. It was horrible, having to go off without him. I hated not knowing where he was going. I'd have been even more upset if I'd known that no-one was going to come for him that day and he would have to spend the night in the school hall. The problem was that Stan was a bed-wetter and no-one wanted to have to deal with that. I don't know why that information had to be given to the prospective foster parents but it was.

Thank goodness, the following day, someone did come to take Stan home and he actually ended up in a very nice house in a much smarter part of town than me and Dennis.

We could walk from the Vesteys' house to see Stan whenever we wanted. It was a longish walk but doable. The only problem was we had to walk past the town cemetery on the way there and my brothers wound me up something rotten with tales of ghosts in the graveyard.

Mrs Vestey was very kind to us. Her husband was a bit of a bully but he wasn't around much. He'd go to work and after work he'd go to the clubs, which were 'men only' in those days. But while Mr Vestey was out, Mrs Vestey had a bit of freedom and used to go out with the Yanks from the nearby air base. I'm sure it was innocent, but Mrs Vestey's American friends gave her presents – sweets and gum and all that, which she passed on to us kids. That was good. I remember that every night at the Vesteys' we'd have cocoa.

One evening, hair-wash night, I went up to the bathroom to wash my hair and when I came downstairs Mrs Vestey told me to comb my hair over a piece of paper. We were racing with the nits! I was absolutely horrified. I don't know where we got them. All the time I was there I had nits, which ended up being one of the reasons that Mum brought us home for good in the end.

While we were evacuated, Dad went all over the place with the Navy. He was on the reserves because he'd been in the First World War. He was only 14 when he signed up back then. He lied about his age and was sent home, but as soon as he was old enough, he tried again. He was desperate to get away from home because his father was a cruel man. Dad told us that he used to hide in the copper so he wouldn't get a bashing.

In the First World War, Dad had ended up on HMS Warspite, taking part in the Battle of Jutland. He brought home a piece of shrapnel. It's only about the size of a salt pot but it weighs a ton.

During World War Two, Dad used to come and visit us at the Vesteys when he was home on leave, bringing lots of chocolate and other gifts. He'd tell us about the adventures he'd had while he was away. He was a wonderful storyteller. Once he told me, 'I've been on the sea and brought home a beautiful parrot. You're going to love it.' I asked him to show me a photo but he said he didn't have one. People didn't have photos very much then. But he told me how lovely this parrot was and I got very excited. I couldn't wait to get back to London and see it. Finally, we got back home and I raced in to see the bird. There was a parrot, alright, but it was a wooden one on a stand. I was so disappointed.

It wasn't easy being back home. While we were in Leicester, I was responsible for my brothers and sort of acted like their mum. When we were back in London it was a different story. Mum was in charge again so I became rebellious and lippy. I got a good hiding many a time.

It seemed like the war would never end but at last we got our victory.

On VE Day everyone was so excited. Everything was decorated red, white and blue. Someone brought a piano out into the street and people set up trestle tables, bulging with food. Dad was home for all the jubilation – on leave perhaps – because I remember going up to Tooting with both my parents.

I didn't stay on at school for long after the war. My headmistress pleaded with my father to let me stay on but he said, 'No, she needs to work.' I went to work as a trainee book-keeper for Swan and Edgar, a department store in Piccadilly. I kept a very neat ledger! Then I went to work in an envelope factory, first in Balham then in Borough.

I met my husband at a family party. A while afterwards, he came by our house, while I was doing the ironing, and asked me to go out with him. I fell in love with his piano playing.

I can't believe it's 80 years since the war ended now. While it was going on, I didn't stop to think about it much. We just carried on. We had to live in the moment. Today's today and yesterday is gone.

26

VICTORY AT LAST

'This is your hour...'

THE LAST V2 FELL ON London on March 27th 1945. Though the V2s had claimed nearly 3,000 lives, ultimately Hitler's Vengeance Weapons had failed in their objective and their launch sites were in the hands of the Allies at last.

On April 30th 1945, Adolf Hitler took his own life in his bunker in Berlin, leaving his generals to face defeat without him. The German high command quickly crumbled. At 7pm on May 2nd, the BBC interrupted its programming to announce that the Germans had surrendered in Italy. Two days after that, they surrendered in Denmark, and the fighting in Europe was very nearly over.

It was not until Monday May 7th that the news Britain had been anticipating for almost six long years finally came, when the Russians and Americans confirmed that the Germans had capitulated at last. At 7.40pm, the BBC once again interrupted its scheduled programme to announce that the following day – May 8th – would be a national holiday - VE Day, for Victory in Europe.

All over the United Kingdom, millions of street parties were quickly convened. Meanwhile, huge numbers of people gathered in Trafalgar Square and all the way up the Mall towards Buckingham

Palace, where Prime Minister Winston Churchill would be joining the Royal Family on the balcony to address the excited crowds. The Royal Family and Churchill were called out onto the balcony several times that day. Churchill gave a speech to the nation, saying, 'My dear friends, this is your hour. This is not victory of a party or of any class. It's a victory of the great British nation as a whole... every man, woman and child in the country had no thought of quitting the struggle.'

Famously, Princess Elizabeth and her sister Princess Margaret, were allowed to leave the palace to join the celebrating crowds. In an interview 40 years later, the by-then Queen Elizabeth II explained, 'I remember we were terrified of being recognised so I pulled my uniform cap well down over my eyes.' She recalled 'lines of unknown people linking arms and walking down Whitehall, and all of us were swept along by tides of happiness and relief.' The princesses danced the night away, incognito – even joining a conga through the Ritz hotel – with Elizabeth describing her brief chance to celebrate the end of the war as an ordinary Londoner as 'one of the most memorable nights of my life'.

Princess Elizabeth's sentiment was echoed up and down the country though, as Churchill reminded everyone in his speech, the Allies were still fighting the Japanese in the Far East. For many families, the war would not be over until August 1945, when the Japanese surrendered and their prisoners, including many British children like Olga Henderson, were liberated at last.

Though the general mood in the United Kingdom at the end of 1945 was optimistic, for many there was still a tough road ahead. The end of the war did not restore to their loved ones those who had been lost on the front line or in the Blitz. It's been estimated that some 13 million European children were orphaned by World War Two. Many more lost one parent. Most of those lost parents were fathers. The loss of a father who was, more often than not, the breadwinner, plunged many British families into poverty.

One war baby whose father would not be coming home was young Londoner Brian Coombs.

Brian Coombs, 83

IT WASN'T JUST THAT I lost my dad in the war, the war meant I never got the chance to know him at all. My father, Stanley Herbert Coombs, was born in Islington in 1920. He was one of three brothers. He and my mother Mary were teenage sweethearts. They got engaged when Mum was 16 and got married as soon as they could.

When the war started, Dad was called up, as were his two brothers. My sister was still a toddler and in 1941, when Dad was told that his regiment – the Beds and Herts – was being sent overseas, they already knew that Mum was pregnant again.

Both of Dad's brothers were sent to North Africa, but Dad was off to the Far East. He wasn't allowed to say exactly where he was going. I don't know if he even knew himself that he was headed for Singapore, but when he left to join the troop ship that would take him there, he promised Mum he would be back in time for the birth of the new baby – me. I was due in April 1942.

I arrived bang on time and Mum was over the moon at the thought of telling Dad he had a son. She must have sent a letter or a telegram via his regiment but she didn't hear anything from or about Dad until eight months later, in the run-up to my first Christmas, when the dreaded black-edged letter arrived, telling her that Dad had died before I was even born.

It turned out that Dad didn't even make it to Singapore. On February 14th 1942, he was killed in an explosion when the Japanese fired on his landing craft as it was just off the coast. He was only 22 years old. Mum was so in love with Dad, that when she found out he'd died, she was never the same again.

Life in Islington was hard enough in 1942, with so many places wrecked by the Blitz, but now that she was a widow, Mum was really on her own, with no money coming in. Dad's parents couldn't help us, so Mum had to move us in with her own mother in Milner Square, between Upper Street and Liverpool Road.

When you go to Milner Square now, you wouldn't believe the way it used to be. Now it's full of big posh houses that sell for millions of pounds. It couldn't have been more different when we moved there at the beginning of 1943. We lived with my grandmother in the ground floor flat of a big house that had been divided into flats. It was not much better than a rat-hole, full of vermin and creepy things that bit me. The walls were always crawling with bugs. The place was falling down. There were at least four families living in there with us.

They were not happy years. Mum had to go to work – she got a job at the Co-op – so she left me and my sister with her own mum, who was an alcoholic. Our grandma was barely able to look after herself, let alone two children under three. She was always in the pub. As soon as we were old enough, she left us to fend for ourselves.

Our clothes were rags and we were filthy. There was never anything to eat in the house. I was hungry all the time. Me and my sister would go picking in dustbins for anything we could find. When I was a bit older, I'd go thieving from shops. I'm not proud of it but it was what I had to do to survive.

Forget Christmas and birthdays. I never even had a card. Everyone talks about the Blitz spirit and how everyone in London pulled together but after the war, people like us were forgotten. When people talk about poverty in London these days, they don't know what they're on about. We were living in a real slum.

My family was wrecked by the war. Mum wouldn't talk about Dad. We saw his parents from time to time but my grandmother on that side was gone in the head through grief. Even after seeing the official letter, she wouldn't believe my father was dead. She never believed it. She died thinking he'd come back at any minute. Her other sons – my uncles – were badly affected by their time in North Africa and the Middle East. They wouldn't talk much about it. Uncle Leslie went off the rails and became an alcoholic. I don't know if that's because of what he'd experienced but it seems likely. I knew Uncle Harry had probably had to kill people but I only asked him about that once. His reaction made sure I didn't ask again.

After the war, the public air raid shelter we used to go to was knocked down to make way for a playground. I started primary school the same year. I found it tough. The teachers were very strict in those days. If you were playing up at the back of the class, they'd throw something at you. One teacher used to throw a bunch of keys. He nearly had my eye out. We were used to corporal punishment.

I didn't get on too well at school. I was alright when it came to reading – I used to help some of the other kids to read – but I couldn't do maths and we had so many changes of teacher, it was hard to know what we were supposed to be doing.

At home, we were all still packed into the one flat together. It got even more cramped after my Mum met my stepfather in 1952, when I was 10. They were both working at the Co-op on Bruton Street then. They got married in 1954. I think they had to, if you know what I mean. So that's how we became a family but not a happy one. My stepdad was quite a bit younger than Mum – 13 years – and he didn't like other people's kids.

With two new people in the flat – my stepdad and my baby half-sister – it was getting too much. My sister had to sleep in a bed with Gran. She got married as soon as she could and went to live with her husband. I was left alone with my stepdad and he got nasty. If I could get together a shilling, I would go and sit in the cinema all day long, just to be out of his way.

It was around this time that I was abused by a man who used to do decorating around the square. I couldn't tell anyone. I didn't have anyone to turn to. Without a dad, I didn't have any male role models to look up to in life. No one I could trust.

I often wondered what my dad was like and whether I was anything like him. I know Dad was musical. He played the piano and accordion. I took after him in that respect. In 1953, I sang on stage at Collin's Music Hall on Islington Green to celebrate the Coronation of Elizabeth II.

Once I was a teenager, I couldn't wait to get out of Milner Square. I did whatever I could to earn a bit of money and I went to night school to try to catch up on the things I'd missed.

I loved music and dancing. I met Brenda at a dance in 1965 and we got married three years later. Like me, Brenda is a north Londoner but we moved to South London when a council house became available there. That's where we brought up our two daughters.

Having a family of my own helped me a lot. I worked hard to provide for my two girls and did my best to be the dad I'd never had. My lovely Brenda was always by my side.

I worked in the City - London's financial district - but I carried on enjoying music, moonlighting as a DJ in the evenings and at weekends. It's through being a DJ that I met the man who set me on the path I'm on now.

It was the early 90s and I was working as a DJ in an east London pub – the Alma in Leyton. There was an old-timer sitting at the bar. He'd had throat cancer, so he had one of those voice box things. It was difficult to make out what he said, so I leaned in to hear him better. This man told me, 'I heard about your father, Brian. How he was killed in Singapore.'

I accepted the man's condolences. 'It was a long time ago,' I said.

'Nearly 50 years,' said the man. 'You should go to Singapore for the 50th anniversary of the Fall.'

'How can I afford that?' I asked.

He told me, 'You can get a grant.'

I had no idea that such things were available. A couple of days later, I found myself in the offices of the Royal British Legion on Pall Mall, filling out the forms regarding my eligibility to join the 200-strong band of veterans and their families who would be flying to Singapore in February 1992. And on February 14th – Valentine's Day – I found myself standing in the Kranji War Cemetery, gazing out over the graves of all the Allied soldiers, wondering how on earth I would find the stone belonging to my dad.

There are thousands of war graves in Kranji Cemetery – tens of thousands – and they've all got the same white headstones. I had no idea where to start. I just broke down. I was standing there crying when this Chinese man came over to see if I was okay. He was one of the men in charge of keeping the cemetery tidy.

'Why are you crying?' he asked me. I told him I was there to visit my dad's grave but I didn't know where to find it. I told him Dad's name and he smiled and told me, 'I know exactly where your father is.'

He took me to the other side of the graveyard. 'Look,' he said. 'Your father knew you were coming today.' When I asked him what he meant, he said, 'Because your father's flowers are the only ones in bloom. Follow me.' Then he led me straight there... it was a plain grave, just like all the others, but this man knew where to find it. There was nothing on it but Dad's name – Stanley Herbert Coombs – and the date he died. But the flowers planted around Dad's grave were blooming and they were the only ones in that part of the cemetery that were. I just stood there for a while. I could hardly believe that I was with my dad at last.

My mother never got to see Dad's grave. All she ever had was a photograph of a simple wooden cross which marked 'graves 14-11', which is all Dad had as a memorial before the stones were put up. Mum died before I went out there. She was only 62.

Seeing Dad's grave changed everything. When I got back to the UK, I decided that I had to do something to support the British Legion, to thank them for the grant they'd given me to go to Singapore. I knew that the Legion's main fundraiser was the Poppy Campaign in the run up to Remembrance Day, so I signed up to collect donations. It was the start of something wonderful for me.

I remember the first time I went out to shake a tin. I put on a suit and pinned my father's medals to the right side of my jacket. I knew it was important to look the part when I was representing the brave men and women in the armed services.

Charing Cross Station became my regular patch and I got very well known there. I've got albums full of photos of the celebrities who stopped to chat and donate in return for a poppy or two.

I met the King, Prince Charles as he was then, several times. The first time was when I was invited by the British Legion to be at Horse Guards on Remembrance Sunday. After the ceremony, we all went into a big marquee, full of important people. Prince Charles came straight up to me to congratulate me on having collected £50,000 selling poppies. We had a nice chat and at the end of it, I told him he'd make a marvellous king and he laughed and told me, 'I'll be dead long before I get the chance.'

The next time I saw him was a few years later. I got a call from the Poppy Appeal asking me if I could do a collection outside the *Daily Mirror*'s Pride of Britain Awards, which were being held in a Park Lane hotel. I stood by the entrance with my bucket as all the celebrities came in. I collected hundreds of pounds that night. Suddenly, there was a commotion as the royal car arrived and Prince Charles got out. He spotted me straight away and said, 'We meet again. You're looking very dapper with all your badges tonight.' He shook my hand and carried on into the hotel but as he was walking up the steps, I called out, 'Excuse me, sir... don't forget you still owe me that fiver!' And everybody burst out laughing. Charles was so surprised that he tripped on the step but he soon recovered himself and called back to me, 'I'll put it in the post.' He's a lovely man and, like I told him, he's turning out to be a good king.

Because I was involved with the British Legion, I was able to go to the Cenotaph on Remembrance Sunday and one year I took Uncle Harry along. That was a very special moment. I was glad to be able to take him there.

All in all, by the time I retired, I had raised more than £1million for the Poppy Appeal.

About 10 years ago, I went to a talk about Milner Square by a film producer who was interested in making a film about the place and the people who lived there. She was going to call it *Through the Hole In The Wall*, which referred to the gap between two terraces on one side of the square. It was a proper tunnel but we all called it the Hole In the Wall.

I agreed to take part in the film. When it came to the day we were recording, there were quite a few people of my generation there. I got talking to one of them while we were waiting and I opened up about the abuse I'd been through. I don't know why I suddenly decided to start talking about it, so many years after it happened. When I opened up, I was told that others had been through exactly the same thing with exactly the same man. It was a big shock, hearing that, and realising how we had all been let down by the adults around us.

When it was my turn to film, the producer took me into a house

– not the house I'd grown up in but one a few doors down that would have had the same layout. It was completely different from what I remembered. The house I lived in had been divided up into flats but over the years someone had bought all the flats in this other house and made it into a single family home again.

It was emotional, sitting in the living room in that beautiful house, seeing what a lovely home someone had made out of it and thinking how different it was to how I grew up just a few feet away. I broke down. I couldn't help it.

While we were filming, the producer of *Through The Hole In The Wall* asked me if I'd move back to Islington and I told her 'no'. Never. Not on your life. Quite apart from the fact that the slum where I used to live would cost millions to buy these days, I would never want to go back to that time in my life.

But the past doesn't leave you alone. You would think that the older you get the easier it would be to put the bad times behind you but the opposite is true. I don't know why. I find I break down quite easily now.

One of the things that upsets me is that I feel as though people like my dad have been forgotten. This year – 2025 – everything was about VE Day. There are people who don't even know that Britain was at war with Japan as well. At the Kranji Cemetery, where my father is buried, there are 24,000 graves. That's 24,000 people who made the ultimate sacrifice. That's 24,000 families that lost a loved one. Hundreds of the people left behind will have been children, like I was, who had to grow up in poverty and suffer abuse like I did because they didn't have a dad. We've been forgotten. Everyone always makes a fuss about VE Day. We should be making a fuss about VJ Day as well.

Standing in Kranji Cemetery, I was overwhelmed with how much I'd lost – how much losing my father had shaped my life for the worse. I know that if he'd been alive, there is no way he would have let us live like we had to in Milner Square. There's no way. If he had come home from Singapore, we would not have been living in that state. My life would have been so different if the war hadn't happened. I don't know if I can ever get past that. But I've got Brenda and my daughters and my beautiful granddaughter now and I feel that I've done my bit with the Poppy campaign. I hope that my dad would have been proud of me.

27

PARENTS WITH PTSD

*'We were two more casualties
of war...'*

WHILE THOSE CHILDREN WHOSE FATHERS were lost in the war could at least perhaps preserve them in memory as eternal heroes, some of those dads who did come home from the war were often so different from the men who had gone away to fight as to be unrecognisable, bringing with them the horror of what they'd seen.

There was a sharp increase in divorce as many returnees found themselves unable to fit back into families that were as changed by five years on the home front as they had been by their time on the front line. The war had absolutely changed the role of women. Those who might ordinarily have given up work upon marriage had remained in the labour force throughout the conflict and the financial independence they'd won meant they no longer had to remain in unhappy marriages to survive.

Some 300,000 World War Two veterans (including 17,000 women) were described as having a physical or psychological disability on their return home. Some of them had suffered unspeakable treatment in German and Japanese POW camps. How could they be expected to return to normality? Especially when normality wasn't what it had been.

Though times had changed since the end of the First World War – the psychological after effects of war were better understood – the 'Keep calm and carry on' ethos that had kept Britain going through between 1939 and 1945 now perhaps made it hard to ask for help. And very quickly no-one seemed to want to talk about the war at all.

It wasn't until the 1980s that Post Traumatic Stress Disorder was finally recognised. Far too late for many of the veterans of World War Two and for their children, like David Taylor.

David Taylor, 86

I WAS BORN IN 1939, just a few days before the declaration of war, though I don't think my birth had anything to do with the outbreak of hostilities.

My memories of the years before 1945 are patchy, given my young age at the time, but when I look at some of the photographs I still have, things do come back to me. There is a photograph of me as a two-year-old in the arms of my mother's brother Ronnie, who is dressed in his army uniform. I'm wearing his tin hat. Shortly after that he was posted to Singapore, where he died on a ship sunk by the Japanese. It's a rare photograph of me with a male relative.

My father, Robert Taylor, volunteered in the spring of 1939 and was among the first to be called up. He wouldn't come home again full-time until 1946. So you could say I spent the first six years of my life not knowing about men at all. I was brought up by my mother, my grandmother and my aunt Amy. It was as though I didn't have a father.

My earliest days were spent at the family home, Beech House, in

Salford near Manchester. It was a large house. My maternal grandfather James Frederick Emery was an important man. He owned cinemas all over the north of England, including one in Manchester that was large enough to accommodate a full-sized orchestra to play along with the films. The house belonged to him.

We were in Salford in December 1940 when the Germans unleashed the Christmas Blitz. I remember having to wear a gas mask and that horrible smell of rubber. I can remember too the thud-thudding of bombs landing far off but mostly I slept pretty well in the cellar, which served as our shelter when the sirens sounded.

I supposed I didn't really know what was going on but it was different for my mother. She was terrified into leaving Manchester. She took me to Cleveleys, 50 miles away on the Fylde Coast, where her parents owned another house. It was much safer there, despite the huge number of servicemen stationed in nearby Blackpool.

With my father away at the war and my grandfather James often in London in his role as MP for Salford West, I suppose I was the only 'man' in the house. My mother and other female relatives doted on me as the only child in the family. I was cosseted and loved. I could do no wrong. I'm sure I was totally spoilt.

I recall standing at the top of the stairs, listening to the three ladies discussing what to do if a German paratrooper knocked at the door. Would they offer him a cup of tea? I can see myself leaping down the whole flight of stairs to land triumphantly at the bottom.

I remember visits from a Mr Bull, who had something to do with the black market, though I didn't know then what the black market was. I remember Christmas in that house and my delight at receiving a kaleidoscope, which quickly became one of my favourite toys alongside a wooden monkey, which climbed up a stick and a wooden toy garage which had one, tiny, battery-operated lightbulb in its workshop.

My aunt Amy, my grandmother's sister, was a particular favourite of mine. She was known as the 'Wigan Nightingale'. She sang light opera and she'd often sing to me. Even all these years later, to hear the 'Merry Widow Waltz' by Franz Lehár takes me back to spending time with that kind lady. She would read to me too. She was very patient on that front. At five in the morning, I would spring out of bed and gather up a selection of my favourite books, then I'd go and knock on Aunt Amy's bedroom door, shouting out 'I'm here', and she was always ready to tell me a story even though she'd only just woken up.

It was Aunt Amy who gave me my love of reading. She brought books to life, giving descriptions of all the main characters, so that I could see them as though I was watching them in a movie. She gave me my first interest in movies too, long before I understood that my family was in the business, with the cinemas we owned. Aunt Amy loved Fred Astaire. Thanks to Aunt Amy, I knew the stories of *Beau Geste*, *Wuthering Heights* and *Random Harvest*, long before I read the books.

I learned how to recite poetry too. My mother was RADA trained and she was very keen on recitation. I would recite J. Milton Hayes' 'The Green Eye of the Little Yellow God', which tells the tale of a soldier named Carew, who meets a tragic end. It would bring tears to the eyes of my doting aunts and all their friends.

My talent for recitation didn't impress my father. I remember him coming home on leave and sharing my bed. I don't know why he was in my bed instead of with my mother. In the middle of the night, he would get up and go to her. He was a stranger to me and I hated it when he came home.

My father was born right at the beginning of the First World War, in 1914. He grew up in Thames Ditton. His mother – my grandma Tay – was a strong matriarch. His father was a mechanical engineer who became a printing machinery salesman. My father followed in his footsteps and became a trained printer.

But while printing was my father's profession, his passion was music. He was taught to play the piano by Grandma Tay, who would later try to teach me to play too. My father was a natural. He could listen to any tune on the radio, immediately pick out the key, and join in on the piano. He was a sublime entertainer.

In 1930, my father formed his own eponymous band, Bob Taylor's Rhythm Boys, and they were soon in demand to play at local dances. His musical talent doubtless played its part in his courtship of my mum, Margaret Emery.

My mother's family was very well-connected. My maternal grandfather was the local mayor before he became Conservative Member of Parliament for Salford West.

With Mum coming from such a smart family, of course her wedding was going to be a major social event. There were 350 guests and an enormous crowd at the church. There was a telegram from Mrs Neville Chamberlain, wife of the then prime minister, wishing the bride and groom well. Thanks to my grandfather's cinema connections, the wedding was even covered on *Pathé* news. My parents honeymooned in Brittany, before setting up home in Reading.

My father joined the Territorial Army in April 1939. He enlisted in the Berkshire Regiment of the Royal Engineers and was called up as soon as war was declared. By October of that year, he had been appointed Acting Lance Corporal, and in January 1940 he set off for France with the British Expeditionary Force. He came back to England to undertake a Motor Transport Course at Chatham before returning to France on the April 7th 1940 as a full Lance Corporal.

My father's second time in France was to be brief. He was one of the men who had to be evacuated from Dunkirk. I think he returned around May 29th. He said he came off the beaches and somehow boarded a destroyer, though he could not remember the name of the ship, nor much about the evacuation. I do know that he sent my mother a telegram, which was a masterpiece of British understatement. It said only, 'Safe in England – Bob'. He would never elaborate on his experiences at Dunkirk and I was too scared to ask him for more details.

Over the following years, my father had a number of promotions. He was posted to the Officer Cadet Training Unit and in 1942, he joined the Royal Armoured Corps, the 79th Division, as a Second Lieutenant. They were known as 'Hobart's Funnies' because the general then responsible for the 79th Armoured Division was called Percy Hobart. My father attended all manner of courses during '43 and '44, from compass reading to explosives.

While my father's regiment saw action on D-Day, I'm unsure whether he was personally involved on that particular day. He was definitely in France shortly afterwards.

He did tell me about being chased across a field in France by a German fighter plane, whose pilot was attempting to kill him. He told me he remembered the noise of the plane's engines and the sound of bullets hitting the earth, as he dived into a ditch to escape. I'm not sure whether that was around Dunkirk or D-Day.

What I do know is what happened next. In March 1945, with the Germans on the run, my father was posted to the Divisional Headquarters of the British Liberation Army. It was a posting that would have an impact on the rest of his life and on the lives of everyone else in the family. Just over a month later, he was among the first Allied troops to go into Bergen-Belsen, the Nazi concentration camp.

Though it was originally established as a prisoner-of-war camp, by 1943, Bergen-Belsen had become a 'residence camp' holding POWs, political prisoners, Roma, 'asocials', criminals, Jehovah's witnesses, gay men and, of course, Jews.

As the Allied and Soviet forces closed in during late 1944 and early 1945, thousands of Jewish prisoners were moved to Bergen-Belsen from other camps closer to the front, such as Ravensbruck, Mauthausen and Buchenwald. In July 1944, it was recorded that 7,300 prisoners were interned at Bergen-Belsen. Eight months later, that number had officially swollen to 41,000 but it's believed that many more went through the camp's gates. Liberated prisoners described going for days without food or fresh water. Disease was rife – dysentery, tuberculosis, typhus. Thousands of corpses lay unburied. The world reeled in horror as reports from the camps hit the news.

On April 22nd 1945, my father wrote to my grandfather, JF Emery, at the Houses of Parliament, hoping he would share the letter with his colleagues there. I still have that letter. He wrote:

Many of you will already have read in the newspapers everything I have to tell you here of the horrors of Belsen Concentration Camp, but because there are cynics among us and also because some of you may not have seen the newspapers, I am going to tell you what I myself have seen...

It is perhaps symbolic that on that road some two miles from the camp, one of our party picked up a whip: a wooden handle with six leather thongs. Signposts were unnecessary. Our nostrils gave us the first intimation of our nearness. Those of you who were at Caen or Le Havre, or any other city which has suffered a shattering bombardment would have recognised the stench.

The first sight I saw while we were still outside the barbed wire was a completely nude woman in the open, who paid not the slightest attention to us, or to the other males around. Rage and filth indescribable, bodies alive and dead, lay everywhere. I entered the camp. A soldier asked me if I could find a doctor as there was a woman imploring him to bring a doctor to her daughter who was dying.

When the woman knew I spoke a little German she begged me to come with her, and find a doctor. I looked into the hut where her daughter was lying and no doctor on earth could have done anything for her. The mother herself had every sign of an early death written on her face...

Not far away I saw two children whose ages I guessed as seven to ten years. Their wrists and ankles were fleshless, their stomachs like balloons. One of these children was playing with a corpse as my son plays with an engine.

I saw a woman endeavouring to wash herself in a water trough. She was one of a line of a dozen, mostly males. Nobody paid the slightest attention to her nudity. I spoke to another woman who was endeavouring to clean herself with a cup full of water. I asked other officers what was their estimate of her age. The lowest guess was thirty-five. She had been taken there two years ago with her parents for listening to the BBC news. Her parents had been shot on the day of arrival and she had been there ever since. She was a German from Berlin. Her age was 17...

I saw only a small part of the whole camp, because my stomach revolted and I had to go.

THIS HAPPENED IN BELSEN IN GERMANY. YET BUT FOR THE GRACE OF GOD YOU MIGHT SUBSTITUTE BIRMINGHAM FOR BELSEN. THIS IS THE WORLD'S THIRD CHANCE. WILL YOU TAKE IT?

It's a vivid account of a terrible moment in history. It's clear that it left a deep impression on my father. He brought a souvenir home from Belsen – that short, multi-strand whip he mentioned in his letter. It had obviously been used. Maybe it is just today's sensitivities, unhardened by war, to think such a thing would not be appropriate as a souvenir. My father kept it in his desk for years. I have no idea why.

A month after my father sent that letter from Belsen, the war in Europe was officially over. I remember VE Day. I was nearly six years old by then. We all had to line up outside school and sing the National Anthem and wave flags. After that, we were allowed the afternoon off. Mum came to collect me, with my little sister in her pram. We children were happy to have an afternoon with no lessons, but I do remember that several of the teachers – all women because the men had all gone to war – were crying as we paraded around the playground. All we children had ever known was rations and gas masks. That was our normal. We didn't understand what war really meant. Or what it meant now that it had ended. But the adults did. Those teachers must have been thinking about loved ones who would soon be on their way home. Or perhaps they were thinking of those, like my uncle Ronnie – who died in Singapore – who would never come home again.

After VE Day, my father remained in Germany, as part of the Liberation Army, travelling to Berlin and Hamburg. Now that the fighting was over, his talents as a pianist and performer were in demand again. He was put in charge of organising entertainment for the troops who were staying on. He was a leading light in the Blackberries Concert party and the Bags of Bull Roadshow, which were the 79th Armoured Division's concert parties. They had a great reputation. My father led the band and they were featured on the Forces Network.

I don't know whether my father was ordered to stay on in Germany after the war ended or whether he volunteered to do so. I think he probably volunteered. By the time he was demobbed in November 1945, he'd served for six years and eight months, out of which he had taken only 90 days leave. I don't know whether that was standard or whether he just didn't want to come home.

He ended the war in good physical shape, with an excellent war record, but something within him had changed. He was moody, bad-tempered and had great difficulty showing any affection – to me at least. He was better with my sisters. To me, he was cold and he was physically intimidating. Whenever I got into trouble with my mother, the first thing I would do is beg her, 'Don't tell, Dad', because I was frightened that he would belt me. He seemed to want to discipline me all the time.

I had no experience of other fathers, and so I assumed that what I was subjected to was the norm. Don't get me wrong, there was very little physical violence. When I was struck, it was usually a clip about the ear with an open hand. Conversely, there was never any loving physical connection. He never touched me, or hugged me, or kissed me. If I had done something particularly noteworthy, like for example, achieving relative success on the rugby field, he would shake my hand, as he would a stranger.

I suppose he thought I was soft, having spent my early years among all those women. He never praised or supported me, no matter how I tried to please him. Mum used to say that he was jealous of me.

Perhaps that's why, at the age of eight, I was sent away to boarding school. Though the school I attended was only four or five miles away from Cleveleys, I was not allowed to come home except during the holidays. I didn't mind. I didn't want to go home.

I went through school, then to college in Guildford to train to be a lawyer. Once I'd left home, my relationship with my father was distant.

He was such an unhappy man, and yet, as is the way with these things, he was surrounded by everything that life could offer, a loving wife, loving children, a stable career, no money worries, and lots of friends to whom he presented a cheerful outgoing personality, but which vanished the minute he returned to the house.

In an effort to cure his depression, he was made to suffer the indignity of electric shock treatment, which further exacerbated his condition. He then tried to commit suicide by accumulating sleeping pills and then overdosing on them, only swift action by the emergency services saving him. In addition, he had to suffer the death of his daughter, my sister Valerie, in a motor accident.

July 22nd 1985 was just a normal day until I got a phone call from the police. First, they made sure I was the person they wanted to speak to. I felt at once that something bad had happened. They told me that there had been an incident at my parents' home. I asked if there had been a burglary but the police officer replied, 'No. It's more serious than that. There's been an incident involving your mother.' In the background, I heard a voice saying, 'Tell him the truth.' And that's when the police officer told me, 'I'm afraid your mother is dead.' What happened after that feels like a dream.

My father had battered my mother to death with a walking stick, then he had gone to the garage and tried to kill himself, using the car exhaust fume method.

When I went to tell my sister Marilyn, I took a police officer along with me. Her reaction was strange. She shrugged her shoulders as if she already knew and said, 'It was bound to happen sometime.' I was ridiculously calm, ticking off in my mind all the practical things that would need to be done. Ridiculous, isn't it, the banal thoughts that go through one's head at a time of shock?

My solicitor friend was with my father for his brief court appearance, where he was remanded in custody. My father did not want to see me. He was sent to Risley Remand Centre in Warrington for a psychiatric evaluation. It wasn't until two weeks later that I finally plucked up the courage to go and see him, after my mother's funeral.

That first meeting was extraordinarily difficult. Can you imagine the conversation? We discussed business, rugby, my work, my children, but talk about an elephant in the room! He seemed only vaguely aware why he was in the remand centre. I decided there was no point talking about what he had done, as it wouldn't change the facts. I didn't want to hear his reasons or excuses. He didn't give any, not even when he wrote to me a few days later. That letter was mainly concerned with material things.

A little later, I visited my father again and this time he did try to explain the reasoning behind his devastating actions. He talked about the difference between his family and my mother's family – his poor background compared to the Emerys' wealth – and how he had always felt in the shadow of his father-in-law. At the time, I took his explanation at face value. He did not talk about his war experiences. Perhaps it was easier for my father to lay the blame for my mother's murder squarely with his father-in-law than relive those days under fire in Northern France or recall the moment he walked into a concentration camp.

I continued to see my father in hospital in the months between his arrest and his death. I continued to see him because of duty. He was my responsibility. No matter what had happened, he was my father.

My father pleaded guilty to manslaughter whilst the balance of his mind was disturbed. During his periods of incarceration, first in secure accommodation and then in various nursing homes, he grew more and more antagonistic towards me, accusing me of stealing his pension, saying that I was, in some way, responsible for his sad plight.

I never understood how damaged he had been by everything he went through. Dunkirk, Belsen and his six years' non-stop service had taken their toll. I believe I lost my father before we even properly had a chance to get to know each other, thanks to his experiences in France and Germany. Now, we would say that he was suffering from Post Traumatic Stress Disorder, but in those days one just put up with it. The British attitude was 'don't make a fuss'. You kept a stiff upper lip and got on with it. But looking at the letter from Belsen again and thinking about the monosyllabic man who came back home after demob, it seems clear to me now that the conditions for my mother's murder were nearly 40 years in the making. My mother and I were just two more casualties of war.

My father died in hospital on December 2nd 1991, aged 77. The cause of his death was emphysema, the same disease which had killed his father. RIP.

Father, I like to think that you might be reading this, perhaps sitting by a stream waiting for that ever elusive salmon to bite, enjoying, at last, the peace you longed for.

I apologise, from the bottom of my heart, for my ignorance and complete lack of understanding, and send you my love.

I expect a kiss when we next meet.

Your son.

28

FORGIVING BUT NOT FORGETTING

Building Bridges

AFTER FIVE YEARS OF WAR with Germany, it was understand-ably hard for many British children to stop seeing Germans as the enemy, particularly when the requirement for all young men to do National Service seemed to emphasise the need to be prepared for another conflict. There was definitely no forgetting what had hap-pened but could anyone forgive?

One war baby who found his attitude to his German peers changed dramatically after he was posted to West Germany as part of his national service was Bob Edwards, who had spent part of the war as a very unhappy evacuee, having been bombed out of his home not once but three times.

Bob Edwards, 93

WE WERE LIVING IN HOUNSLOW in West London when the war started. It was quite a large house we lived in. Dad was a dentist and he had his surgery and waiting room downstairs. He was a very good dentist, with lots of loyal patients but in September 1939, Dad joined up, to fight for king and country. He felt that was his purpose in life. He left Mum with me and my sister Marge, who was five years younger than I was.

We weren't evacuated initially. We stayed where we were. I carried on going to school. When the Blitz started, it seemed exciting. Me and my mates would go looking for bombed out houses on our way to school. We used to look for shrapnel we could show off in the playground. That was an everyday occurrence.

We did have an Anderson shelter at home but Mum didn't like to use it, thinking the damp in there gave her bronchitis. Our grandparents lived fairly locally and they had a Morrison shelter in the dining room. If we were at their house, then Marge and I used to be bedded down in that. Otherwise it was used as a table.

We were bombed out. We were actually bombed out three times. The first time was when a high explosive landed nearby. Luckily it didn't demolish the house, but it did take all the window frames and doors out and brought the ceilings down... It also brought the wardrobe down on top of my sister's cot. Thankfully, the strong sides of the cot saved her.

We couldn't stay in the house, of course. We had to go to our grandparents, walking over there just as we were, still dressed in our nightshirts, with our pet dog and one toy each for me and Marge.

It should have been terrifying but I must have blanked it out because the only memories I've really got are of the aftermath, as we wandered about trying to find the cat, stuff like that. We stayed with our grandparents until the house was rebuilt and we could move back in. Then of course it happened again.

The second time we were bombed out, Mum went back to the house during the day to find a few belongings and found it had been looted. The electric and gas meters had been broken into, because they were coin meters, and all the money taken. In some ways, that was worse than the bomb damage, knowing that someone had stolen from us while we were so vulnerable. Mum had to find the money to reimburse the companies all the same. By the broken gas meter we found a heavy metal truncheon. The thief was obviously ready to hit anybody who interrupted while he was taking the money. So we had that nastiness to contend with as well as being out of our home.

I was evacuated very briefly between then and the third bombing. I think it's because I didn't get on with my grandfather, who was a tram driver. I was sent down to Newnham in Gloucestershire to stay with two dear old ladies. They were sisters, never married, and they lived above a sweet shop. I was fortunate in that respect.

Ironically, the afternoon I arrived, Newnham got its one and only bomb of the war, off-loaded by a German bomber on its way back home.

Newnham was very different from London. I remember the old milkman coming round with the horse and cart and the milk churns. We used to go out with a jug. The River Severn was at the bottom of the garden. But nothing ever happened in Newnham. Apart from that one time, they weren't bombed. There was nothing there that the Germans could have aimed at, whereas at home, we were near the Great West Road, and they were after the big factories along there. On one occasion they got a factory that produced face powder and everything got covered in that.

I was very resentful of being sent away because I had more things to occupy my days up in London. Being sent to two little old ladies, no man in the house. It was a real change. I remember having a bath in a tin bath in front of the fire. At home we lived in quite an upmarket house, because it had the bell push in every room, so you could call for the servants. And so there were quite a few rooms. And we had a big garden that I used to enjoy playing in.

At home, I was always occupied and I had my friends as well. There was a big grassy area opposite us where we could play Cowboys and Indians and stuff like that. And there was a factory nearby that used to produce tractors. We used to go and annoy them there. I would always hang around the garages, wanting to learn about cars, and I've been a car nutter ever since. Being evacuated there was just nothing to do. That's possibly why I started misbehaving. I turned on all the taps in the local school and flooded the place. I wasn't allowed to go again. I'm pretty sure I must have done that deliberately, hoping they'd send me home.

Being evacuated was a big change for a lot of children. They felt that they'd been sent off and abandoned. I'd never been away from my family since I could remember. And my sister not being with me as well made it seem like I was being punished somehow. All the same, I didn't get to go back to London until 1944, just in time for the V1s and V2s.

On July 29th 1944, Dad was home on leave for the weekend. It was Saturday night. Marge and I were in bed but Mum and Dad were still downstairs in the kitchen when, shortly after 11pm, a doodlebug cut out right over our house, then plummeted into the back garden of The Hollies, just a few yards down the road. The noise was deafening. When I woke up, my bedroom looked like a building site. The air was full of dust and the floor was covered in broken glass and plaster. For a moment or two, I couldn't hear a thing, then suddenly I heard Mum shouting, 'Where are the children?'

Down in the kitchen it was chaos. The sash window had been blown in and somehow ended up falling over Mum's head so that the frame was around her neck. Meanwhile, the kitchen door had fallen on Dad. By a miracle they were both okay, if a bit scratched up.

While Marge and I stood there, Dad suddenly asked if anyone fancied a cup of tea. We thought he was mad but he went into the scullery and came back out with three cups of tea and a pint of Guinness for himself. We drank our tea then, once more, set out for Gran's. That single doodlebug damaged 630 houses.

Dad had joined the Royal Ulster Rifles infantry. He used to do a lot of motorcycle work and also worked on testing tanks.

During the war, Mum worked in the accounts department of Purdey, the gun people. When Dad came out of the army, Purdey's offered him the finance to start a new dentistry practice. He would have made a fortune. He was a dental mechanic, able to make false teeth and everything, but he was too proud. He decided that if he couldn't do it by himself he wouldn't do it. So he worked for Purdey, as an engraver. Later, he was one of the first dentists to join the National Health Service.

I was glad to have Dad back. We were very close and very similar people. He was very clever with his hands and enjoyed putting things together and mending things, which I do now. Rather than go out and buy something, I'll find out why it went wrong and if I can put it right I will. Same with repairing cars.

While Dad was away, we'd sometimes had a family living with us, renting a couple of the rooms to help Mum with the money. That was another thing Dad used to do: if anybody was down and out, he'd invite them home for the night. We had one who actually stole things. That didn't go down well, but that was Dad. If he met anyone worse off than himself, he had to help them out. I think it was because he served in the First World War. He never told us what he saw out there but it probably was the reason he was the way he was.

When I was 18 I was conscripted but because I was an apprentice, I didn't do my National Service until I was 21 when I went into the army.

I joined the Royal Electrical and Mechanical Engineers (REME) out in Germany, first in Duisberg, then Wuppertal. It was the early 1950s and Germany was still rebuilding. I don't know what I expected the German people to be like, after my childhood experiences of being bombed, but I knew at once that they were just ordinary people, like we were. There shouldn't have been a war.

During my apprenticeship, I'd trained to be an electrician on lift gear but there was no call for that. I said that I liked working on cars in my spare time so I got drafted in as a vehicle mechanic. We were attached to the Durham Light Infantry. I used to follow the convoys and pick up the vehicles that broke down.

We had Germans working with us in the workshops and we all got along fine. That said, the younger Germans really didn't like us. When it was May Day, we were told not to go out of camp in uniforms. The only vehicle that was allowed out was the ration truck which occasionally got attacked and turned over. But the people of our age, or just a bit older than us, they were just the opposite. If we were on our own in a pub, they'd call us over to sit with them. They asked us to join them on New Year's Eve. It was the youngsters that were really against us. The people who were our age and older were fine.

We used to go to the American Air Force bases and go into their PX club. It was like another world. You could buy cars, fridges, anything in a PX club. All we had was a NAAFI where you could get a cup of tea. I quite liked it in the army actually. I would have stayed in if I had no family.

Having gone to Germany post-war and met Germans and been welcomed by some of the older generation, I started to see that the differences are quite artificial and they're whipped up by politicians.

While I was over there, I went to Belsen. The people who lived around the camps must have known what was going on. I think they were too terrified to stand up to the Gestapo, because they were brutal. But it was all based on one man, wasn't it? One man's thoughts. You get some charismatic person telling people that their problems are due to other people and they fall for it. If we got a politician like Hitler here today, would we follow him?

The most valuable lesson we learned from being children during wartime is to be kind to others, really, and to do unto others as you would have done to yourself.

29

WAR'S LEGACY

'People didn't think about the psychological effects of war... least of all on children...'

IF BRITAIN'S WARTIME SPIRIT WAS exemplified by a single phrase, it would have to be 'Keep calm and carry on'. It recalls the British tradition of the 'stiff upper lip'. No panicking, no fuss, no complaining.

With the war over, the British people might have thought, to quote the song, that 'Happy Days Are Here Again'. But as they grew up playing on bomb sites, without parents, or around fathers traumatised by their service on the front line, how could Britain's war babies leave the war behind? What invisible damage had been done?

Even as early as December 1939, renowned psychologist John Bowlby, whose work on attachment styles in childhood is still widely revered today, was concerned about the long term effects of the evacuation of very small children. Together with his colleagues, Emanuel Miller and DW Winnicott, Bowlby wrote a letter to the British Medical Journal, drawing attention to the possibility of problems down the road. The psychologists were of the view that, 'There are dangers in the interference with the life of a toddler which have but little counterpart in the case of older children. Evacuation of older children has been sufficiently successful to show, if it were not known before, that many children over five can stand separation from home and even benefit from it. It does not follow from this that the evacuation of smaller children without their mothers can be equally successful or free from danger... chronic delinquency, mild behaviour disorders, anxiety and a tendency to vague physical illness can often be traced to such disturbances of the little child's environment, and most mothers of small children recognise this by being unwilling to leave their little children for more than very short periods.'

As we know, Bowlby et al's concerns did not stop the evacuation of very small children from going ahead. And it does seem as though they might have been proved right. Twenty-first century studies into the long-term effects of World War Two evacuation, such as that by James SM Rusby and Fiona Tasker, who interviewed 870 evacuees, discovered that those who were under six years old at the time of evacuation were found to be at greater risk of depression and anxiety as adults.

Even those children who spent the war in relative safety, at home in familiar surroundings, might be exposed to second-hand trauma. The idea that the children of Holocaust survivors could be affected by their parents' trauma, is well known. Less well recognised is that World War Two military veterans might pass on their trauma. In 1986, psychologist Robert Rosenheck studied five families where the father was receiving treatment for PTSD. He wrote that, 'For some of the veterans' offspring, it was as if they were ... constantly embroiled in a shared emotional cauldron.'

Many war babies decided not to examine the effect the war might have had on them but for Violet Morris, the question lingered until the answer was triggered by a chance conversation with her mum, many decades later.

Violet Morris, 85

I WAS BORN IN THE summer of 1940, just as the Battle of Britain began. My parents were living in Sidcup by then but Mum was evacuated to High Wycombe to have me (lots of the maternity hospitals had been moved out of London for safety) and that's where we stayed, with a very kind host family, until I was old enough to come home. The woman with whom we'd been lodging stayed in touch with Mum. She was very kind. I think people liked to think they were contributing to the war effort by helping out in some way.

Sidcup is about six miles out of London but it is not far from the river and what were then the munitions warehouses at Woolwich Arsenal. We lived in a new-built house on the estate of Lord Waring, who owned nearby Foots Cray Place. The Palladian mansion house was requisitioned at the beginning of the war and used as by the Thames Nautical Training College.

Our house was one of several houses, built in the late 1930s, which were arranged on a crescent, with fields behind. One of my earliest visual memories is of a barrage balloon floating over a field.

My father, Fred, had joined the army but because of his tuberculosis he wasn't sent overseas. Instead, he was based in Shropshire, looking after the armaments in that part of the country. He'd go around on a motorbike, checking they were in good order. Mum and I were left alone in Sidcup.

I was very small during the Blitz but I do remember hearing the air raid siren when we were out and about later in the war. It must have been around the time of the Little Blitz, in early 1944. We had a Morrison shelter – a steel frame with a top that looked like a table. That fitted in our back room. I remember when I was about three years old, being in the Post Office near our house when the siren went off. The adults bundled me under the counter until it was safe to come out again.

Though it was usually pretty quiet during the day, we would hear the planes over London at night. The Germans would follow the Thames into the city so they would pass close by. We could see the searchlights and hear the ack-ack guns defending London's docklands.

One night, a bomb hit the house across the street from us. It was a 1930s chalet style house and half the roof was destroyed. Another bomb fell in the garden of another neighbour. Fortunately, the garden was long and the bomb fell at the end of it so the house itself wasn't damaged. Word soon got round and it wasn't long before all the children who lived in the street were there, peering down into the crater. The blast from that particular bomb melted the decorative glass panel in our front door. It didn't shatter, because it was held in place by thin strips of lead. Instead it sort of bubbled inwards. I rather liked it like that. Thankfully that was all the damage our house suffered.

Sidcup wasn't an obvious target for air raids so I think that most of the bombs that fell on the town were dropped by German pilots on their way home. All the same, two bombs was enough. Mum felt particularly nervous with Dad being away so we started to spend a lot of time with my aunt and uncle, and my cousins, who lived on a farm in nearby Swanley. Now it's a suburb of London but Swanley was proper countryside then.

Because we didn't have a car – and couldn't have got the petrol to run one anyway – Mum would put me in my pram and walk all the way to her sister's. It was a three-mile journey, along the A20. Every so often we would pass a big billboard. When I was three or so, I started to recognise that the squiggles on the billboards were words. That's how I started to learn to read. Pretty soon, I knew that one of the signs said 'Gordon's Gin Stands Supreme'. I would recite it loudly and often at inappropriate times.

Mum obviously felt safer being further from Woolwich Arsenal. The farmhouse was an interesting place, built of green-painted corrugated iron in the shape of a church. To begin with, we would all sleep in the very middle of the house but as the war went on, my uncle decided we needed a proper shelter and built a dugout in the farmyard. It wasn't luxurious – it had dirt walls – but it was big enough for us to sleep in comfortably. There were bunks for the children and a separate curtained off part at the end so that the adults could have a bit of privacy. I loved it. It felt to me like camping. I felt very safe as long as I had my teddy bears Tederica and Edgar, who was named after an uncle who had been a despatch rider in World War One.

Once, when Dad had been home on leave, we went with him to Paddington Station to wave him off again. I think it was around 1944, so I would have been almost four years old. It's a moment that has stuck in my memory. I remember that our train into London ran close to the river and the skyline was full of magnificent cranes. When we got to Paddington, the station was full of men, soldiers from everywhere. I saw Sikh army men in their turbans. Black American soldiers as well. Mum, having waved Dad off to Shropshire, was enjoying the attention.

Suddenly, I spotted a great big soldier, who was eating a bun and holding another one.

'Mum, look!' I shouted. 'He's got two buns.'

The soldier heard my exclamation and turned to ask me, 'Would you like one?'

Of course I said, 'Yes, please.'

Mum was mortified. For years after she would recount the story, telling me, 'I was so ashamed.' Even not long before she died, she said to me, 'You know, when you took that bun...' But I was just so happy to have it. We didn't have many treats. And it was an amazing moment for me because I had never seen so many soldiers. I don't think I saw anybody weeping as we said goodbye. There was a sense of safety, security and purpose around the men we saw at Paddington that day.

Though I obviously felt I needed that bun, we didn't go hungry thanks to being on the farm, which had vast fruit orchards. We also benefitted from my uncle helping to plant up our garden in Sidcup. We were well stocked for fruit and veg. We children would pull radishes straight out of the ground and eat them, dirt and all.

The farm was arable but there was a horse which drew the plough when we first went there. Later, my aunt and uncle had tractors and I fell in love with the driver, who let me steer the tractor around the farmyard. When he went and got engaged, I was heartbroken!

Towards the end of war, a number of German POWs came to work on my aunt's farm. I was allowed to mix and chat with them. I remember one in particular, called Emile, who was very kind to me. He was about my father's age. Perhaps he had children of his own back in Germany.

I think at that stage, most people in Britain could hardly believe that a German was an actual person but meeting Emile and the others, I got to see a different side to them.

On VE Day and for VJ day too, we hosted a garden party. Because our house was at the end of the street, we had an especially big garden. Food was laid out on a long table and from somewhere someone had brought a donkey so that the children could have rides. Since the party was taking place in my garden, as I thought it was, I decided that I should get first ride. In the end, I didn't get a chance to ride the donkey at all. I was very put out.

The war was still on everyone's mind when I started at school in September 1945. At break and at lunchtime, the boys would play at being fighter pilots. They'd take off their coats and tuck the sleeves in so that they could wear them like capes, then they'd turned their caps backwards to make them look more like fighters pilots' leather helmets. Dressed like that, they would zoom around the playground, making engine noises, with their coats flapping like wings behind them.

Hitler was still very much the baddy in our playground games and I learned a number of unsuitable songs about him!

Post-war, Dad was posted to Egypt, Iraq and Palestine. What he saw in Palestine broke his heart. He was still away with the army when my baby brother was born in the winter of 1945. Because there was no-one who could take me for the full first 10 days after his birth, when Mum had to stay in hospital recuperating. I was shipped between four different people. The last person to have me was a work friend of my mother who didn't have any children of her own. I was pretty miserable, having been away from Mum for so long. I was only there for one night but I'll never forget having breakfast the following morning. Mum's friend asked me what I would like. She had a box of bran flakes and I decided that I would like to try them. Unfortunately, I didn't like them at all. When I said I didn't want to eat them, Mum's friend got very angry, telling me, 'We're all short of stuff and you're wanting to waste food.' I couldn't wait for Mum to get home, even if things were very different now that I had a brother. I was soon feeling pretty resentful.

When Dad was finally demobbed and was able to come home to meet his new son, Dad took me into London on a day trip to see St Paul's and I saw how much of the city had been laid to waste.

Years later, Mum was musing on how different my brother and I had been as small children. She told me that my brother was a very easy baby while I had been difficult and fractious. 'Your brother was a little ray of sunshine,' she said. 'But you were always bolshie.'

Finally it clicked for me. It wasn't just a matter of us having different personalities, 'Mum,' I told her. 'He wasn't going through a war with you. He didn't experience all that fear. It was just you and me on our own and you were very scared.'

Mum's reaction to the V1s was a good example of the difference between my brother's childhood and mine. I was about four at the time the doodlebugs started and I remember my mother telling me, 'They're very noisy, so you can hear them coming but if the sound stops and it's very close, it's probably going to fall on the house.' When that was the sort of thing I was hearing, of course I was going to be a difficult child. I might not have entirely understood what I was being told but children can sense tension.

Childcare in the 1940s was influenced by people like Dr Truby King, who advocated very strict routines. The child must be fed every four hours, regardless of whether they're hungry or not. They must be placed in their own room very early on. You shouldn't cuddle them too often. That sort of thing. There was no space for an individual child's needs or a parent's instincts in Dr Truby King's world. I think my mother had read the books. I was raised very strictly.

Mum had never thought of the most significant dissimilarity between my upbringing and my brother's. She hadn't considered how she might have been a different mother to my brother than she had been able to be to me with the war causing everyone so much anxiety. But people didn't think about the psychological effects of war in those days, least of all on children.

Though I had met German POWs on my aunt's farm, I didn't go to

Germany until many years later. In 1960, I went to the Netherlands with a friend and we hitchhiked as far as the German border but we didn't cross over. It was a strange moment. It was around the time that the Russian president Nikita Khrushchev was in the UN, banging his shoe on the desk. I was so upset, being far from home, when that happened. I was sure that another war would break out and I would never see my parents again.

Shortly after that, I went to India with a friend to volunteer at a school for Tibetan refugees. We went by boat from Marseille, through the Suez canal, and I remember spending part of the journey sitting in a wardrobe with a young man who was on his way to join the French Foreign Legion. He had amazing eyelashes. I was in India for about a year and hearing about the experiences of the Tibetans was transformative for me. It's where I first started to get interested in Buddhism, which would be important to my view on war and conflict later on.

A few years after that, my friend went back to India a second time and I joined her for part of the journey overland. This time, I did have to go through Germany. It was more than 20 years after the war but I was still full of trepidation as we got close to the German border. What was beyond? Wolves and bears and people of unspeakable cruelty? That's what five years of being at war does to your thinking. We went to Munich and drank beer. We slept in people's farm outbuildings on straw. Eventually we got to the Yugoslav border and I had to turn back to make sure I was in London in time for the start of the new term at teacher training college. I had thought I would be able to get a lift back with another bunch of Brits but there was no-one going my way. It was £16 to get the train back to England from the Yugoslav border and I only had £12, so I had no choice but to hitch.

The first person to stop for me was a German woman, who did not like the idea of a young woman hitchhiking on her own at all.

She was determined to look after me and stayed with me until I was able to flag down a British Land Rover which was going my way. She was really lovely and her kindness stayed with me. It made me realise that the Germans were just like us in so many ways. They didn't have horns. They weren't green!

All these years after World War Two ended, I still find my heart races when I hear a helicopter. Though I didn't think I could distinguish the sound of the German planes from the RAF planes as a child, I realise now that the sound of a helicopter does remind me of the German planes flying over at night and I can't relax until I'm sure what's going on. I have to know where the noise is coming from.

The Germans have tried to educate successive generations about the war. Our attitude in Britain has been different, though it seems to me we only 'won' by the skin of our teeth. We haven't examined what the war really meant.

In India, working with the Tibetan refugees, I heard a lot about the Chinese invasion and it was chilling. Learning about Buddhism made me realise that war is about mind and where our minds are. We all have dark corners in our minds and hatred. Some people recognise those dark corners, some people don't. I know otherwise good people who are totally unforgiving of certain things. Evil wanders around in various quantities. I have good days but I've also had days when I've been so angry that I feel I could destroy anything. I have miserable days. People get stuck in bad thoughts. That's the danger.

It's easy to get whipped up into hatred if the people around you are caught up in it too. Hitler fomented hate with great speeches. 'This is our fatherland...' He made the Germans feel that other people were at the root of their problems. He dehumanised the 'enemy'. That sort of thing still goes on today. In places like North

Korea, people are placed in terrifying, dehumanising situations but they still have human feelings. Leaders like Putin and Kim Jong Un are sending ordinary people to do their bidding.

It's hard to feel sorry for psychopaths, such as Hitler must have been, but I try to have understanding because these people's minds are in hell. They are in hell because they can create these terrible situations and have no sense of compassion for anyone else. How do you get out of that? How do you live with the damage you've created? It goes on and on. War is always unspeakably ugly.

EPILOGUE

'...Unity and peace...'

A LITTLE MORE THAN A year after the end of the war, on June 8th 1946, London hosted a day of celebration. It began with a victory parade down the Mall with representatives from most of the Allied Nations (Russia, Yugoslavia and Poland were missing). Later, crowds lined the Thames to watch a flotilla including the Royal Barge. In the evening there was an extravagant firework display. That same day, King George VI sent a message to the children of Britain. The King wrote:

'Today, as we celebrate Victory, I send this personal message to you and all the other boys and girls at school. For you have shared in the hardships and dangers of a total war and you have shared no less in the triumph of the Allied Nations.

'I know you will always feel proud to belong to a country which was capable of such supreme effort; proud, too, of parents and elder brothers and sisters who by their courage, endurance and enterprise brought victory. May these qualities be yours as you grow up and join in the common effort to establish among the nations of the world unity and peace.'

The King's hopes for his young subjects were a lot to live up to but the children of World War Two would do their best. In the immediate post-war years, they continued to bear the material hardship of life in battle-ravaged Britain with equanimity (sugar and sweets were still rationed in the UK until February 1953). They would do their national service. They would work to rebuild their country and uphold the values the Greatest Generation had given so much for.

However, the Silent Generation, as they were dubbed by *Time Magazine* in 1951, did break from its parents in many ways. They were the world's first teenagers, with a cultural scene that spawned 'rock and roll'. They're the generation of The Rolling Stones and The Beatles, of James Brown and Aretha Franklin. Their poster boys were hell-raisers like Warren Beatty and Jack Nicholson. Their leading ladies were Elizabeth Taylor and Jane Fonda, who both brought politics to Hollywood. They were a generation of activists. In 1975, the British Silent Generation overwhelmingly voted to become part of Europe.

In general, the Silent Generation has a clear-eyed view of the war years, lacking the rose-tinted nostalgia one might expect. Yet perhaps there is still a generational blind spot about the war's impact.

It's interesting to note that for many of our interviewees, it's only in recent years that they have begun to understand just how much World War Two might have shaped them. Eight decades after the conflict ended, some are experiencing their first flashbacks to frightening nights in cramped underground bomb shelters. Others find they can no longer tell the wartime stories they've happily told their whole lives without breaking down as they speak. Some are finally finding compassion for their emotionally distant parents and asking forgiveness of their own children for the damage done by insisting on a 'stiff upper lip'.

All our interviewees were shaped by their experience of the war just as surely as those adults who went to the front. All of them hope most ardently that their grandchildren and great-grandchildren will be spared the same.

As Catherine Russell, director of Unicef, wrote on X at the end

EPILOGUE

of 2023, 'Children don't start wars and they have no power to end wars, but they are the ones who suffer the most.'

At the time of writing, new conflicts rage in many corners of the globe. A new generation of children is spending nights in bomb shelters, becoming refugees and losing their loved ones. Perhaps listening to the voices of those who were children during World War Two, and examining how their lives developed in the decades that followed, can help us to better understand how to support this new band of war babies in the years to come.

Chris Manby and Simon Robinson
London, 2025

ACKNOWLEDGEMENTS

THE AUTHORS WOULD LIKE TO THANK:

Jim Gill, Katerina Lygaki and Cathi Holden at Felicity Bryan
Associates. Clare Fitzsimons, Christine Costello, Nick Webster
and Claire Brown at Mirror Books

Rosemary Ball
Geoffrey Bourne Taylor
Mark Carroll
June Collins
Brenda Coombs
Brian Coombs
Dot Clowry
Doreen Dancer
Bob Edwards
Mark Gabriel
Olga Gretton
Ann Hay
Olga Henderson
Vera Hogg
Andy Hull
Derek Hull
Jean Kent
Jackie Kershaw
Sylvia Lee

WAR BABIES

Tony Lee
Ann Manby
Nicholas McCarthy
Doreen Middleton
Beryl Morgan
Alison Muir
Norma Nimmo
Moya Oxford
Bill Rhodes
Dan Rhodes
Vivienne Rhodes
Phil Schwarz
Cynthia Smith
Maud Smith
Alice Taylor
Bunny Taylor
Jeannette Tomlinson
Victoria Tomlinson
Mark Williamson

AUTHORS' NOTE

WHEN WE SENT OUT A request for interviewees we were overwhelmed by the response. Constraints of time and distance meant we were unable to get to everyone who kindly offered to speak to us and we must apologise in advance for any resulting gaps in our coverage of those wartime events that most affected the children of Great Britain. A subject so all-encompassing needs more than a single book.

Some of our interviewees are published writers. You can read more from David Taylor in his memoir, *Beloved Ghosts*, and his novel, *Amanda*. Olga Henderson's wartime memories are collected in her book, *In The Shadow Of The Rising Sun* (Mirror Books).

THE SILENT GENERATION
IN PHOTOGRAPHS

Ann Hay

Bunny Taylor

Derek Hull

The Dead End Kids

The War Effort

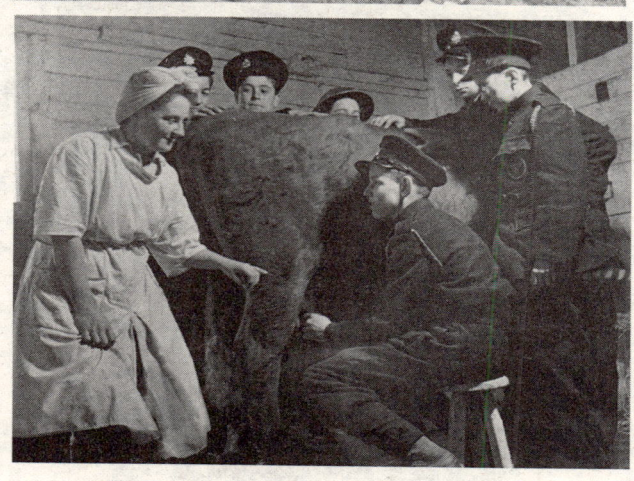

Olga Henderson

Jeannette Tomlinson

The Coventry Blitz

Cynthia Smith

Jackie Kershaw

David Taylor

Rose Brown

Fifteen-year-old Rose Brown, of Marcia Road, Walworth, has taken the place of a milkman who was called up for the Force

Freddie Harrison

Freddie Harrison, six, and his sister Winifred, three, whom he saved from the ruins of their home during the Blitz

Brian Coombs

Alan Hogg

Certificate of Honour

N.E.S.
THIS
CERTIFICATE
OF HONOUR
IS AWARDED TO
GRINDLEY AVE
SAVINGS GROUP
IN RECOGNITION OF SPECIAL ACHIEVEMENT
DURING THE
WINGS FOR VICTORY
NATIONAL SAVINGS CAMPAIGN 1943

I EXTEND MY THANKS TO ALL CONCER...
...N THIS IMPORTANT NATIONAL SER...

Letter:

39 Grindley Ave No 2
Savings Group

WINGS FOR VICTORY

WINGS FOR VICTORY WEEK IS
NEAR,
BUY YOUR SAVINGS STAMPS
FROM HERE,
AND YOUR HUSBANDS, SONS AND
DAUGHTERS,
WILL GET HITLER AT CLOSE
QUARTERS,
MANCHESTERS AIM £11,000,000
POUNDS
WILL BUY MORE PLANES TO
BOMB HITLERS GROUNDS
P.T.O.

Newspaper clipping:

A Great Little
Fellow

WHILE cycling to deliver
newspapers, Alan Hogg,
aged 13, of Grindley Avenue,
Thorton - cum - Hardy, was
knocked down and killed by a
bus.

A member of Barlow Hall
Methodist Church, and a cub of
Alan was the secretary of
Grindley Ave. Savings
No. 2 Group, and in the
last 12 months he col-
lected over £425. He also
collected for the Blind Children Society and helped at
the gathering of salvage. In
an interview with the City News
a senior member of the Savings
Group described Alan as one
of the gave most efficient,
hard-working little chaps I have
had the pleasure of knowing."
Alan was a pupil of New
Central School, Wythenshawe,
and his brother, a Petty Officer
in the Royal Navy, has arrived
home on compassionate leave.

285

Similar Mirror Books Titles

In The Shadow Of
The Rising Sun
Olga Henderson

With Chris Manby

In February 1942, nine-year-old Olga Morris and her family were in Singapore when the city fell to the Japanese Imperial Army in the biggest defeat in history of the British Forces.

Turned back at an evacuation ship's gangway as the bombs fell, Olga and her parents and siblings were forced to take their chances and hide out until, captured by Japanese soldiers, they were sent on a forced march to the notorious Changi Prison.

It's a story of great fear and deprivation; of a childhood utterly lost to conflict. Yet moments of humour and camaraderie also live on in Olga's memory.

Similar Mirror Books Titles

Century Sisters:
Our Hundred Years
Patricia and Jean Owtram

With Chris Manby

The best-selling authors of Codebreaking Sisters, Pat and Jean Owtram, take us back in time once again with recently rediscovered diaries and letters from the '20s and 30s that paint a vivid picture of their childhood at Newland Hall in Lancashire's Lune Valley.

Here they lived with their parents Bunty and Cary Owtram and younger brother Bob, supported by a fascinating cast of cooks, maids and groundsmen, all presided over by 'Grandboffin', the sisters' indomitable grandfather.

Using contemporaneous correspondence, diary entries and their 21st century reflection, *Century Sisters* tells the story of a bygone era with inimitable Owtram style and flair.